CONTENTS

Thanks are due to the Estate of the Earl of Derby
for a financial contribution towards the costs of publication.

Preface

Lancashire in the nineteenth century usually means cotton and the industrialis-ation and urbanisation it brought. But much of the county remained rural and agricultural. The contrast may seem to be between towns undergoing rapid social and economic change, and a countryside retaining its traditional form. In this book Dr Mutch shows that it was not so. He demonstrates how his chosen area – agricultural south-west Lancashire – underwent a transformation that closely complemented the changes in the towns.

The expanding industrial economy created a demand for food that enabled agriculture to grow, especially in contiguous areas. It became as market oriented as the cotton market itself, responding to new demands and re-organising production to meet them efficiently. This affected social relations. For as long as growth continued, it was possible to maintain the facade of the traditional dependence between landlord, tenant and labourer, but behind this, it was ordered by the penetration of the market. This was made clear by the response to agricultural depression when it arrived in the late 1880s. Landlords attempted to retain their hegemony, but had to face collective organisations among tenant farmers, who themselves found their labourers striking in 1913.

Dr Mutch's account brings to life and explains a phase of Lancashire history previously little known. His readers will find it difficult to travel again across the rather featureless landscape of south west Lancashire without contrasting it with the dramatic lives of those earlier inhabitants.

Oliver M. Westall

Acknowledgements

My interest in rural history was the result of an attempt to discover more about my Aberdeenshire farming ancestors. During that process I came across Ian Carter's fascinating work on farming in North East Scotland, which turned my attention to the countryside of Lancashire. Once I started researching the nineteenth century rural society of the county I became particularly intrigued by the south west plain, which contradicted so many of the received notions I had of rural history. This study is the presentation of the results of that fascination.

One theme whose importance did not strike me when I began the work was the centrality of the small farmer. In the mid-1970s it was still assumed that the march of progress demanded even bigger units of production. Now, after the twin blows of world economic crisis and over-production, doubts have begun to creep in. The observations in what follows on the role of the small farmer have a new relevance. However, with the reassessment of the way production is organised has come a romanticisation of the countryside. The trend towards organic production in smaller units brings with it the danger of a nostalgic obsession with the "natural", a renewal of the old myth that in the countryside one will find the peace and social harmony that is lacking in the conflict-ridden city. I hope that a deeper investigation of nineteenth-century rural society will show that in at least one small but important sector of rural England change and conflict were built in. Further I would argue that while production is organised for profit subject to the dictates of the market, such conflict is always possible. Finally, the farm worker is so often seen as the powerless victim of circumstances, unable to share in the prosperity of the industry and first to suffer when depression arrives. The history of the farm worker in south west Lancashire shows that this was not always the case, and I hope shows that it is not inevitable in the future.

I have many people to thank for their help and advice in the research which went into the writing of this study. I owe a great deal to Mike Rose, not only for his guidance whilst supervising my doctoral thesis on which so much of this work is based, but also for his encouragement in the following years. I would also like to thank the following for helpful criticism and support: Ian Carter, Andy Charlesworth, Andrew Bullen and Oliver Westall. I should like to record my appreciation of the efforts of the staff of the following institutions: Lancashire Record Office, Preston; Liverpool Record Office; Public Record Office, London; the *Ormskirk Advertiser*; local and national officers of the National Union of Agricultural and Allied Workers (now the Agricultural trade group of the TGWU); and to the following who kindly allowed me to consult papers in their personal possession: Mrs S. Jacquest of Ormskirk and Mr and Mrs Whitlock-Blundell of Crosby Hall. I must also thank all those farmers and farm workers who put up with my questioning and rewarded me with so much fascinating material. Finally my greatest debt is to my parents: without their support at a crucial period this research would probably never have been started and I trust the dedication of this study to them will in some way repay them.

A. Mutch

Plate 1: A Lancashire moss cart, with wide wheels to prevent it sticking into the soft surface of the reclaimed land

Introduction

The south west plain of Lancashire is one of the most fertile agricultural districts in Britain. Massive crops of vegetables are grown in deep, reclaimed moss soil. Yet this area is virtually ignored in the histories of both agrarian change and rural society. Perhaps this owes something to the industrial nature of the farming, which has not produced the classic English countryside of calendar and chocolate box. Nineteenth century visitors found it a dismal prospect. A publicist for the new watering resort of Southport looked on the bright side in 1839, expressing the hope that "we may soon expect even this bleak and dreary wilderness to put on a fruitful and healthy appearance".[1] Whatever progress was made during the next 15 years failed to impress an American visitor, Nathanial Hawthorne. He found the area "as flat and uninteresting a country as I ever travelled . . . I have not seen a drearier landscape, even in Lancashire".[2] A French visitor in the same year, 1855, admired the enormous productivity of the area's farmers, but could not find a good word to say about their surroundings. With horror he described

> a most gloomy climate, continual rain, a constant cold seawind, besides a thick smoke, shutting out what light penetrates the foggy atmosphere; and lastly the ground, the inhabitants, and their dwellings completely covered with a coating of black dust.[3]

This bad press may explain why the area is by-passed in the historical record. The mental image conjured up by school book history may also have something to do with it. The North is the land of cotton mill and mine, the South of corn and yokels. There is a bias towards the southern experience in much rural history which is as much a social as a geographical bias. The picture which is drawn is of a society divided into landlords, large farmers and landless labourers. Of course, reference is made to the north and to small farmers, but these seem almost by way of asides. An illustration of this bias may be seen in two recent works on rural England during the period under consideration.

G. E. Mingay's *Rural Life in Victorian England* is the latest work to attempt a broad popular sketch of the subject. There are five references to Lancashire in the index. Turning to the text, it is found that only one of these actually refers to farming, the other four being concerned with either fishing or rural industry. The farming reference is to Robert Neilson, perhaps the most untypical of all the county's farmers. He was an interesting person, a large farmer with a practical mechanical genius, who certainly deserves mention. But Lancashire was dominated by small farmers, who find no mention. In fact Mingay's chapter on farmers is for the most part concerned with large landholders, for along with a lack of treatment of Lancashire goes a similar lack of treatment of the small farmer.[4]

The same strictures can be applied to one of the best works to appear on the subject in recent years, *Village Life and Labour*. This work is of course concerned with the labourer, so its lack of mention of the small farmer is understandable.

1

Less understandable is the almost total omission of the north of England, and with it the farm servant. Once again, the majority of the small number of references are to fishing rather than to farming, the only reference to the latter being to the absence of women field labourers, in itself a debatable point. Thus the otherwise excellent piece on "The place of harvester in nineteenth century village life" is in fact about *south eastern* harvesters.[5]

This bias can give an unfortunate picture of the development of British agriculture. Economy and social structure exhibited striking differences from region to region. Steps have been made towards this, notably in the outstanding work by Ian Carter on Aberdeenshire.[6] In that work he pointed out the need for concrete analysis of the development of economy and social structure in specific areas. The present study attempts such an analysis for this much neglected part of rural Britain.

It is necessary to outline some of the theoretical assumptions that fuel the analysis that is presented here. One is that rural society is not exempt from the constant change that is a feature of capitalist economy as competing producers attempt to find new ways of realising profit. Change may not seem as rapid or as drastic in its consequences as in industrial areas, but it is nonetheless a reality. It is necessary to stress this point as the countryside has often been seen as the antithesis of the town. In this scenario the countryside stands for stability and harmony as against the conflict-ridden, urban world of change and upset. This ideological argument was in evidence as much in the nineteenth century as today, when it seems to underpin much of the hankering after the "good life" of unspoilt rural peace. M. E. Francis (the pseudonym of a member of the Little Crosby gentry) presented this picture in her *In a North Country Village*, published in 1897. Not only had the village escaped the scourges of the present; it had also avoided the profound changes that had affected the rest of rural England in the eighteenth and nineteenth centuries and had remained "unchanged to all intents and purposes for several hundred years".[7] This view of the villages of south-west Lancashire as unchanging islands of harmony is reflected in the description of the 1981 reissue by C.U.P. of Margaret Penn's classic *Manchester Fourteen Miles*. This claims that

> The seemingly short distance from the capital of England's cotton industry was nonetheless the distance between one world and another. "Moss Ferry" was a village which belonged to the old agricultural order, that is before cotton arrived. It had hardly changed, economically or socially, for hundreds of years.[8]

I will argue that, on the contrary, the nineteenth century saw dramatic changes in the rural economy and society of the area.

The other assumption that underlines the study is that rural society was composed of classes with fundamentally different interests. At its crudest this can be demonstrated by the following contrasts. In 1860 Charles Scarisbrick died leaving a fortune estimated at three million pounds, having enjoyed an income approaching £100,000 a year from his lands in and around Southport.[9] Some five years earlier Christopher Richmond, a farmer of Thornton, had his will proved at Chester as being worth nearly £10,000.[10] In 1859, in Little Crosby, "a man of

2

the agricultural class . . . considered himself well paid and a big wage if he got ten or twelve shillings for his week's wage".[11] The vast differences that these sums indicated are ones that no blurring of class lines can obliterate. Of course, material difference does not automatically bring a realisation of differing interests. The growth of awareness of these differences, and the conflicts that this insight brought, are major themes in what follows.

There has recently been some questioning of the general assumption that there was no peasantry in nineteenth century England. It has been argued that in fact substantial numbers of small producers survived and that they played an important role in blurring class lines.[12] There is no doubt that too much emphasis has been placed on the large farmer, and that in Lancashire small farmers dominated numerically and economically. Close examination of the large "progressive" farmers beloved of contemporary observers shows that some of the criticisms of their lack of practicality by small farmers had some foundation. Small farmers were the backbone of the agrarian economy. This fact has important social consequences, as the social distance between farmer and labourer was often much less than in other areas.

It seems inappropriate, however, to describe these small farmers as constituting a peasantry. Most did not own their holdings, although this does not seem a particularly strong objection. More crucial was the employment of labour. The south west of Lancashire was an area of labour-intensive cultivation and most farmers holding over 50 acres employed some outside labour. In addition farmers produced for the market and not for subsistence. This meant that they all, large and small, practised similar forms of cultivation and this gave them a broad common identity. The local newspaper's assessment seems accurate:

> They are more of capitalists than of labour, and make the business a scientific one, with ample capital, liberal use of manure, the best seed and cattle and abundance of labour, by which, if at all in these times, farming is made to pay.[13]

This is not to say that farmers were a homogeneous mass with identical interests, but the term peasantry seems an inappropriate one.

The area under consideration is the flat, south-west plain between the rivers Mersey and Ribble, centring on the market town of Ormskirk. With a population of 6,183 in 1851, the town failed to take advantage of the prosperity of local agriculture. Thus there was little alternative employment to agriculture within the area itself. However, it was ringed by fast growing industrial towns, from Preston in the north through Wigan and St. Helens to Warrington, Widnes and Liverpool in the south. These settlements, and the growth of industries such as mining on the fringes of the area, meant that many employment opportunities were close at hand. The main physical attribute of the area was the vast mosses which when drained became excellent arable land. However, at the opening of the nineteenth century these were still largely waste and the demands of the mushrooming towns could not be satisfied by local farmers. The transformation of the area's agricultural economy to meet these demands is the first theme of what follows. I then look in turn at the impact that these massive changes had on farmers, landowners and farm workers. Finally come the events that led to

3

conflicts of interest firstly between farmers and landowners and then between workers and farmers. Very roughly, the period of transformation is placed between the end of the Napoleonic Wars in 1815 and 1850. From mid-century to the late 1880s was the "golden age" of prosperity for local farmers. The breakdown of this and the strains it caused occupy the years from then to the outbreak of the First World War.

Notes
1. R. Cocker (pub.), *A compendious history of Southport, a favourable and fashionable watering place in the parish of North Meols*, Wigan, 1839, p. 12.
2. Nathanial Hawthorne, *The English Notebooks*, New York, 1941, p. 397.
3. Leone de Lavergne, *The Rural Economy of England, Scotland and Ireland*, Edinburgh, 1855, p. 261.
4. G. E. Mingay, *Rural Life in Victorian England*, London, 1977, pp. 57, 82, 107, 110. For Neilson see below, pp. 14-15.
5. R. Samuel, (ed.), *Village Life and Labour*, London, 1975, pp. 13, 79, 104-6, 115.
6. I. Carter, *The Poor Man's Country, Farm Life in North East Scotland 1840-1914*, Edinburgh, 1979.
7. M. E. Francis, *In a North Country Village*, London, 1897, p. 4.
8. Margaret Penn, *Manchester Fourteen Miles*, Cambridge, 1981.
9. M. Girouard, *The Victorian Country House*, Oxford, 1971, p. 61; *Gentleman's Magazine*, vol. 209, 1860, p. 100.
10. Lancashire Record Office (L.R.O.) Preston, Act Books of Wills proved at Chester, 1855.
11. Thomas Barnes, *Changes from 1860 to 1910 along the Banks of the River Mersey* (hereafter Barnes, *Changes*), typescript at Crosby Hall, p. 59.
12. See the discussion by Mick Reed, "The Peasantry of Nineteenth Century England: a Neglected Class?", *History Workshop Journal*, 18, 1984, pp. 53-71.
13. *Ormskirk Advertiser*, 2 January 1879.

1

The Transformation of Farming

(a) Preparing the ground

Across much of England, and crucially in those areas which dominate our agrarian history, enclosure has been seen as the necessary precondition for agricultural improvement. The individual farms with enclosed fields clustered around the farmhouse, now seen as the quintessence of the English landscape, were carved out of the great medieval open fields cultivated on a collective basis. Such a forced shift in property relations was not necessary in Lancashire. Here farms had to be carved piecemeal out of the moss. This process continued relatively unchanged physically, but under the greater control of the landlords. Traditionally farms had been held under long leases, often for generations. This meant that farming continued in the old inefficient ways and gave little chance to improve yields, either of produce or rent. Landlords thus sought to move to agreements for a definite number of years.

This process was a slow one which spread over many years. Leases were allowed to run their course and the land then taken in hand, and relet on new terms. The old leases, classically for three lives, were still being extended in the mid-eighteenth century. In 1767 Thomas Eccleston "agreed with Helen Ashcroft for £36 to add her Son Robert's life (aged six years) to hers".[1] Thus as late as 1869 on the Derby estates "the defects are chiefly in farms that have lately come out of long lease, or are still in it . . . the houses are mean and in bad repair".[2]

Some of these leases included payments in kind or "boons", chiefly of labour, in addition to money payments. Thus in 1769 Thomas Eccleston agreed to lease "Henry Hollands" to Henry Lyon for £130 and five days' shearing.[3] Such boons were still being demanded as late as the 1840s. A nice example of the conflict between market forces and customary obligations was highlighted by the report of Sefton's agent in 1845 that "there has been considerable difficulty in obtaining Boon straw lately on account no doubt of its high price. I have threatened the defaulters to make them pay for the deficiencies which has had the effect of bringing in three loads last week".[4]

The first move away from these leases was to agreements for seven years, many based on those granted in Norfolk. These sought to force farmers into a particular form of cultivation. In Thomas Birchall's agreement of 1784 he was to "consume all the produce, or for every load of hay sold to find two good loads of dung and for a load of straw one good load of dung".[5] The extent to which some landowners would attempt to direct their tenants' farming methods can be seen in the practice on the Speke estate which gave rise to Binns' complaint that the conditions imposed were such as many repectable men would object to; they are tied to the mode of management, even to the number of cattle they are to keep, having no scope for judgement or discretion of their own, as to the best mode of cultivating their farms, – being thus mere machines.[6]

Once the system desired was firmly in place, the rules were relaxed. Freedom of cultivation became the hallmark of the Lancashire farmer. On the Sefton estate, it was reported,

> Mrs Birch can do what she likes with her land and with the produce of it. Her business is to make the farm profitable in order that she may pay a heavy rent and a heavy wages bill, and realise a profit for herself; and the liberty which she has results in the very highest fertility of which the land is capable.[7]

Some farmers enjoyed this freedom with no formal contract whatsoever, and were proud of their independence. "I have no agreements with Lord Derby for my farms", wrote James Martland, "and we neither of us wish for any".[8]

The new freedom of the agreements brought new opportunities to landowners. One was a much greater ability to weed out ineffecient or inadequate tenants. On the Sefton estate there was a regular assessment of tenants, and those who failed to meet the standard set were evicted. In 1845 twelve tenants were removed. John Willacy of Netherton, "not a steady sober man", had rent arrears of £222. James Bradshaw of Altcar, with a rent of £40, had incurred arrears of £79. In the agent's opinion he "might have done well but for his drunken habits. I think it would be very desirable to weed him out". However, those "weeded out" were not only the drunken or the incompetent, but also those who failed to match up to the estate's idea of good farming. Henry Harrison of Orrell, for example, "is a decent man but he has no Capital and says he never had". Henry Shacklady of Kirby was "a steady person but he lacks ordinary energy". Regular payment of rent was no safeguard:

> It may appear somewhat harsh to part with Mrs Blanchard so long as she pays her rent, but in strictness it is not so – the Farm would never improve under her management, in fact it would deteriorate, and this objection applies as well elsewhere on the estate as at Croxteth, and therefore I think it is wise in your lordships refusing her application to be placed on another Farm.[9]

This strict attitude might be relaxed for special reasons. In Knowsley "the Tenantry here are, or have been allowed to remain undisturbed, and to jog along in their now old course, because they were old tenants, & well known at headquarters".[10] But improvement brought its casualties as well as its favoured tenants and the successes whose stories were loudly trumpeted in the agricultural books and journals. One such casualty was John Wood of Halliday Moss Farm, Rainford, who hanged himself on receiving notice to quit from Lord Derby.[11]

New agreements also offered landlords the ability to put some of the cost of improving their land onto their tenants in return for lower rents. At Eccleston William Culceth was to take a farm "the largest Feild [sic] all covered with Gorse" and was to leave it "Green side upwards and clear of Gorse". A reference to "Jos. Edwards new close on Catchall Moss" appears to indicate that tenants were beginning to take in raw moss.[12] According to one account moss was reclaimed in strips by a number of farmers in patches detached from their main

6

farms. This cooperative reclamation meant that "the expense and labour of reclamation was distributed among a number of farmers instead of being confined to one or two on whom the burden would have been too great".[13] When times were harder towards the end of the nineteenth century some farmers used their forefathers' creation of new farmland as a weapon in their struggle for lower rents. "My Grandfather took the land out of the heath and built this house", wrote James Ball of Banks to his agent "so that I do not like to leave the old place".[14]

Much work was also required on existing farms before they could realise their true productive potential. One holding in Huyton before improvement was described as

> a lost impoverished farm with wretched winding roads, great dips, ponds, ditches and sprawling stretches of weedy lands . . . In the centre and round the farm were huge sprawling ditches, and there were dykes and hillocky lumps everywhere.[15]

The universal remedy for these ills was drainage. The Manchester and Liverpool Agricultural Society was in no doubt as to its importance, organising in 1854 a draining match with prizes for gangs digging and laying drains "in the best and most expeditious manner". The Society's inspectors were pleased to note in 1857 that "there is no falling off of this useful work", and continually encouraged farmers to continue draining in their annual reports.[16] The two usual ways of carrying it out were either that the landlord found materials and labour, the tenant paying a percentage in addition to rent, or that the landlord found the materials and the tenant the labour. Leone de Lavergne found that on Lord Derby's estate, "A body of nearly one hundred labourers, under a special agent, has been employed to drain his lands. The farmers are required simply to cart the draining tiles; and upon completion of the work, pay, in addition to their rents, five per cent on the outlay".[17]

To take advantage of the newly drained land a lot more work had to be done. Many fields were small and divided by hedges which were "broad, crooked, and full of oak trees and old stools, with deep ditches". Clearing these meant that "a considerable land is gained . . . besides giving more air to the corn crops, affording less harbour to vermin and making the fields more convenient for cultivation".[18] Later fears about this practice were foreshadowed by Lord Stanley's warning at the 1869 Ormskirk Agricultural Show that "it is bad economy, to say nothing of destroying what of natural beauty the country possesses, to keep a field without protection for cattle or crops, for the sake of gaining a few additional square feet of ground".[19]

Important as all this activity was, it pales into insignificance besides the enormous areas released by the draining of the peat mosses. Early attempts to achieve this met with little success. Celia Fiennes commented at the end of the seventeenth century that

> I avoided going by the famous mer named Martin mer that as ye proverb sayes has parted many a man and his mare . . . it being very hazardous for strangers to passe by it. Some part of yt mer one Mr Fleetwood has been at ye Expence to draine so as to be able to use

7

the ground for tillage, having by trenches and floodgates with banks shut out ye waters, yt still kept it a marsh and moorish ground.[20]

Marten Mere was four miles by two at its greatest extent and Chat Moss extended to over 1000 acres in 1795. A combination of factors was required to tackle these massive areas: technology, markets and capital. The crucial problem for landowners was that the scale of investment required for large scale reclamation was out of proportion to the surplus that could be generated by their existing holdings: in Fletcher's opinion, it was "not until the end of the eighteenth century did landowners find themselves with surpluses for investment".[21]

The source of this surplus was directly or indirectly industrial capital. One result of booming industry was the mushrooming growth of Lancashire towns. Manchester grew from a town of 75,000 in 1801 to a city of 303,000 in 1851; Liverpool in the same period grew from 82,000 to 376,000. The combined population of eight of the major urban areas of South Lancashire was by 1851 over one million. Yet the county's farmers were chronically unable to match the increased demand this represented until well after the Napoleonic Wars. Holt complained in 1795 that "the corn raised in Lancashire would not support the inhabitants more than three months in the year". According to him, "capital, labour, ingenuity and attention are in this county diverted from agriculture". His main concern was the attraction that the towns held for labourers: "who will work for 1s 6d or 2s a day at a ditch when he can get 3s 6d or 3s a day in a cotton works, and be drunk for four days out of seven?"[22]

The key to the realisation of the value locked in the mosses lay in the diversion of some of the surplus being generated by the industrial economy. This could occur in a number of ways. The most direct, of course, was through those landowners who exploited the resources on their lands, like the Bridgewater estate. It was not necessary, however, to directly soil one's hands in manufacture or commerce. The control of strategic land could be immensely profitable. Derby owned much of Bootle and realised its potential by slowly releasing land for building. The rental of the Knowsley estates was £31,881 in 1800. It increased by leaps and bounds over the next 85 years, rising to £95,199 by 1850 and £231,130 by 1885. In 1876 60% of this income was generated from the "industrial" portions of the estate. The most productive of these was Bootle, with a rental in that year of £70,668.[23] The Scarisbrick fortune was founded on the success of Southport. Its expansion brought Charles Scarisbrick an income of some £100,000 a year. A third way for industrial surplus to be chanelled into the land was for its owners to buy their way into the ranks of the gentry. This was the trajectory of Richard Watt. He made his fortune on the Jamaica plantations and used it to purchase the Speke estate. As we have seen he then used it to radically improve the estate. Finally urban capitalists could take the task on directly, although they did not meet with conspicuous success. The drainage of Chat Moss was first attempted by a partnership of William Roscoe of Liverpool and Mr Wakefield, a sugar refiner. After Roscoe's bankruptcy in 1820 the work was taken over by Baines, the owner of the *Leeds Mercury*.[24]

The details of the gradual reclamation of the mosses can be found in Fletcher's

8

account. It was a slow process. In 1869 Sefton's Kirby estate still contained about two square miles of moss. In the same year, however, Derby could write with pleasure that "the aspect of the country in this quarter is gradually changing; roads are straighter, fences neater, fields larger, new plantations making a show; improvement is being vigorously pushed". (He continued regretfully, "but the neighbourhood of so many coalpits will always prevent Rainford from being attractive to the eye".)[25] Further improvement was required, however, if the productive potential of the new land could be properly exploited. A dramatic change in the quality of communications was required.

(b) The spread of communications

"The roads in every direction are execrable", complained one resident in 1844.[26] Development was hampered by poor communications both within and into the area. It was ringed by rivers made difficult to cross by low marshy banks, mosses and moors. The only easy points of access were at Warrington, Wigan and across the Ribble at Penwortham. "Preston is reckon'd but 12 miles from Wiggon", wrote Celia Fiennes, "but they exceed by farre those yt i thought long the day before from Liverpoole; it is true to avoid many mers and marshy places it was a great Compass I took".[27] Within the area mosses lay across travel routes and streams had to be crossed by ferry. At Bretherton "the waters of the Lostock frequently rise, so as to cut off the whole population from the opportunity of uniting with their neighbours in the public worship of Almighty God".[28] Farmers were unable "for the want of good roads to get manure or clay on land early enough in Spring".[29] Thomas Eccleston's new iron plough, bought in Scotland in 1767, had to be sent by sea via London to Liverpool.[30] If produce was to be sold in the booming urban markets and farmers be able to take advantage of new technology it was essential that communications should be improved.

The first major development came not with the improvement of roads but with the growth of a canal system. This began with the improvement of navigable rivers, the Mersey and the Irwell from Manchester to Warrington and the Douglas between the Ribble and Wigan in 1736 and 1742 respectively. The first canal to be opened was the Sankey at St Helens in 1755, and from then until 1819 a number of canals were built which opened up considerable areas of the county. By their founding Acts many carried limestone and manure free. The Mersey and Irwell had no tolls on dung, marl or manure to be used on lands within five miles of their courses.[31] The Lancaster canal, built to connect Wigan and Kendal and opened in 1819, carried coal north and limestone for agricultural use in the south on its return journey.[32] The influence of canals was, however, limited to a narrow belt on either side of their course. The development of railways was to have a far deeper effect.

Lancashire was of course a pioneer in the building of railways with the opening of the Liverpool and Manchester line in 1830. The first to serve the south-west came in the form of the Liverpool, Crosby and Southport line in 1848. This line was known locally as the Farmers' Line, "as most of the Farmers that were in a position to take shares took as many five pound shares as they could spare the money for".[33]

Few farmers would feel the benefit of railways as directly as W. H. Carter of Carrington Moss, who had his own private siding, but all farmers would feel the impact of the system, even those without direct contact.[34] To a certain extent it nullified the advantage of proximity to urban markets, as Lord Sefton's agent pointed out in 1844; "it is unquestionable that they [railways] tend to a great degree to equalise the value of land consequently impairing the advantages possessed by such a locality as the neighbourhood of Liverpool".[35] In particular it encouraged a switch to liquid milk production. Milk was first sent to Manchester by rail in 1844 and by 1893 76 per cent of its daily milk requirement arrived in this manner, a total of 17,387 gallons.[36] The railway companies provided special waggons for its carriage, and farmers were not slow to take advantage. The opening of the West Lancashire line in 1882 saw a shift by farmers in its vicinity from cheese making to liquid production for the Liverpool market.[37] Similarly, the opening of a station at Midge Hall near Leyland in 1868 encouraged the growth of market gardens sending their produce by rail to Liverpool and Preston.[38]

The improvement in communications that came with the growth of the railway system was the final factor in the transformation of the farming of the plain. It enabled farmers to get their produce to the voracious urban markets. In turn, the massive increase in production had required a change in the way farms were rented to give landowners much greater control over their tenants. By means of this control the area under cultivation was greatly increased. Landowners also intervened directly by channelling industrial surplus into the work of mossland reclamation. All these processes were spread over a considerable period of time, but one can see the movement gaining momentum after the Napoleonic Wars and the decisive transformation occurring by the 1840s. By then the agriculture of south west Lancashire was firmly tied to satisfying the needs of its massive urban neighbours.

Notes
1. L.R.O., Scarisbrick papers, DDSc 127/3, Book of Memoranda begun in 1765, Thomas Eccleston, 11 January 1767.
2. Liverpool Record Office (Lv.R.O.), Diaries of the 15th Earl of Derby (Derby Diaries), 13 August 1869.
3. Scarisbrick papers, DDSc 127/3, 22 November 1769.
4. L.R.O., Sefton papers, DDM/6/128, 22 April 1845: DDSc 127/3, 22 November 1769.
5. *Ibid.*, 10 January 1784.
6. Jonathan Binns, *Notes on the Agriculture of Lancashire*, Preston, 1851, p. 145; *Journal of the Manchester and Liverpool Agricultural Society (J.M.L.A.S.)*. Speke tenants won the prize for the best farm in the following categories: over 150 acres – 1854, 1855, 1856, 1867; 100-150 acres – 1855, 1856, 1857, 1865; 50-100 acres – 1854, 1855, 1856. Lv.R.O., Speke papers, 920SPE, 18/5, Agreement with James Kerr.
7. *Agricultural Gazette*, 16 July 1877, p. 67.
8. DDSc 79/1/(59), letter to the agent, 24 December 1896.
9. DDM 6/140, 12 July 1845, 6/165, 6 June 1847.
10. Lv.R.O., Derby papers 920DER(15), Hale Correspondence, 4 May 1863.
11. *Orms. Adv.*, 17 May 1867.
12. DDSc 127/3, 31 October 1771, 6 May 1766.

13. J. A. Taylor, *Mossland Farming in South West Lancashire*, University of Liverpool M.A. thesis, 1949, p. 78; cf. J. A. Taylor, *Studies in South West Lancashire Agriculture*, London, 1964, p. 3; J. Grundy, "Allwood House Farm, Astley", in W. G. Hoskins (ed.) *History from the Farm*, London, 1974, p. 130; and J. Lunn, *Shade and Shadow*, London, 1950, p. 21.
14. DDSc 79/1(54), 9 October 1895.
15. *Preston Guardian*, 13 August 1898.
16. *J.M.L.A.S.*, 1854, p. 20; 1857, p. 25.
17. De Lavergne, *op. cit.*, p. 263.
18. *J.M.L.A.S.*, 1856, p. 43.
19. *Orms. Adv.*, 12 August 1869. *J.M.L.A.S.*, 1856, p. 43; 1861, pp. 47, 19; 1868, p. 47.
20. C. Fiennes, *Through England on a Side Saddle in the time of William and Mary*, ed. Mrs Griffiths, London, 1888, p. 153.
21. T. W. Fletcher, "The Agrarian Revolution in Arable Lancashire", *Transactions of the Lancashire and Cheshire Antiquarian Society*, 72, 1962, p. 122.
22. J. Holt, *General View of the Agriculture of the County of Lancaster* (1795), Newton Abbot, 1969, pp. 71, 211, 213.
23. Derby Diaries, 2 January 1886, 1876 (n.d.).
24. Fletcher, *op cit*.
25. Derby Diaries, 15 August 1869, 21 May 1869.
26. DDM/6/116 7 September 1844, T. Weld Blundell to Lord Sefton.
27. F. Walker, *Historical Geography of South West Lancashire before the Industrial Revolution*, Manchester, 1939, pp. 10-15.
28. Central Reference Library, Manchester; Archdeacon Rushton's Returns, vol. 77.
29. DDSc 79/1/33, 18 July 1849, W. H. Talbot to Charles Scarisbrick.
30. DDSc 127/3, 15 January 1767.
31. C. Hadfield and G. Biddle, *The Canals of North West England*, Vol. 1, Newton Abbot, 1970, p. 16. See also Holt, *op. cit.*, p. 197; L.R.O., Hesketh papers DDHe 70/27, John Parker to Liverpool Canal Company enclosing lists of tenants in Rufford, Tarleton, Hesketh with Becconsall, Much Hoole and Wrightington exempt from paying dues on manure.
32. Hadfield and Biddle, *op. cit.*, p. 182.
33. Barnes, *Changes*, p. 57.
34. *Journal of the Royal Agricultural Society of England (J.R.A.S.E.)*, 11, 1910, p. 259.
35. DDM 6/112, 20 August 1844, R. Ledger to Lord Sefton. On the benefits accruing to landowners from railways crossing their lands, with particular reference to Sefton, see J. R. Kellet, *Railways and Victorian Cities*, London, 1969, pp. 180-3.
36. J. Burnett, *Plenty and Want*, Harmondsworth, 1968, p. 21; *Journal of the British Dairy Farmers' Association (J.B.D.F.A.)*, X, 1895, p. 141.
37. *J.B.D.F.A.*, XXV, 1911, p. 21; X, 1895, p. 68.
38. C. A. Carruthers, *Leyland: a study of Agricultural and Industrial Development*, Manchester University B.A. Geography thesis, 1959, p. 25.

2

Farming and Farmers

(a) Muck and markets

The extent of the needs of Lancashire's urban centres can be seen in a brief look at Manchester's demand for food. By 1895 its daily consumption of milk was 22,851 gallons.[1] The Smithfield vegetable market at Shudehill was purchased by the city in 1846, reroofed in 1853, and constantly expanded to meet the continual pressure on its space.[2] In 1873 the newly formed Manchester Farmers Club was complaining of the lack of cover available to farmers bringing their produce for sale. The result was damaged goods and discomfort for the carters who had been travelling for two or three hours to arrive at the market by 6 a.m. The lack of an office in which to complete transactions was also bemoaned, as it led to accounts being settled in the nearest public house.[3] By 1897 the market covered four and a half acres but this was still inadequate, with produce stacked in neighbouring streets. Over 230 loaded vehicles were known to have arrived between midnight on Friday and 6 a.m. on Saturday, whilst two railway companies estimated that in 1896 they had carried 33,000 tons of produce into the city. As four major companies ran into Manchester the total railborne traffic must have been still higher.[4]

Human needs were not the only ones that required fulfilling. Nineteenth century cities housed large numbers of animals. Their demand for feed, coupled with human demand, stimulated farmers to greater productivity; the waste they produced made such productivity possible. The national population of horses in towns has been estimated to have been over a million in 1891.[5] At that time around 20 million tons of goods a year were moved by 16,000 horses in Liverpool.[6] In 1893 the Manchester Carriage and Tramway Company claimed to be the largest single buyer of horses in the north of England. Its 385 tramcars required 3,583 horses to pull them, all replaced over a five year period.[7] Very few of these horses were supplied by Lancashire farmers as the horses they bred (with the exception of those in the Fylde) were too light for town work. Farmers derived their benefit from these enormous numbers of horses in the sale of feed and access to large quantities of manure. A horse in a Liverpool stable would produce four tons of droppings a year which, as F. M. L. Thompson points out, "if properly made up with straw litter was the basis of 12 tons of good manure; but which if left about in the streets was just four tons of nuisance".[8]

There were also large numbers of cattle in the dairies of Liverpool and Manchester. In 1890, for example, there were 57 registered cowkeepers in Manchester with 664 cows.[9] Like the horses, cattle produced a great amount of manure and required large quantities of food.[10] This provided the basis for the

12

exchange which took place every year when farming operations were at a low ebb. Hay was cut out of the stack in 56lb trusses and carted into the towns in loads of one and a half tons. There it would be sold at hay and straw markets or, better still, exchanged directly for manure at a stable such as that of the Pendlebury Carriage Company. Some farmers would undertake yearly contracts for the removal of middens. Samuel Cook of Linacre had such a contract with a stable of 94 horses, yielding 376 tons of manure. The result was the use of enormous quantities of manure by the farmers of the south-west plain. John Wright of Croxteth Park applied over 1,200 tons of Liverpool manure to his 326 acres each year. Such applications sustained high yields and enabled land to be intensively cropped year after year.[11]

The tailoring of agricultural systems to this urban demand was by no means an immediate reaction. It has already been seen that the ideas of Norfolk had considerable influence. These stressed a balanced system in which the produce of the farm was consumed by stock, which in turn produced manure to fertilise the land. It took some time to realise that this was inappropriate to south-west Lancashire, where far more value could be realised by selling all the farm's produce and buying in cheap urban manure. This system saw the bringing of most of the farm under tillage, leaving only a small proportion in permanent pasture. That this took some time can be seen in Dickson's comment of 1815 that, "in the south west part of the county, there is a very large intermixture of grass land, so as to render it less properly a grain district".[12] This is confirmed by an analysis of estimates given for nine parishes in 1849, which indicates that the proportions of land under arable and permanent grass were almost the same at 47.6 and 47.95 per cent respectively.[13] By 1870 a considerable shift had taken place, as only 21.89 per cent of the area under crops and grass was returned as being permanent pasture.[14] There were, of course, variations within the region. Altcar, with its meadows along the Alt, still maintained a figure of 41.71 per cent, whereas in Melling the proportion was as low as 5.42 per cent. Grain crops, with 33.2 per cent of the total, claimed the highest proportion, followed by 22.77 per cent under green crops (potatoes, cabbages, etc.) and just over 20 per cent under temporary grass. The usual rotation followed was green crop after grass, then wheat, followed by oats or barley and finally three years under grass.

Oats was the most important grain crop, occupying 13.39 per cent of the total area. This was largely sold for feed in the towns. The rich land produced large quantities of straw which was almost as valuable for feed or bedding. Wheat was still grown on a significant scale, although possibly declining in importance. In 1870 it covered 12.82 per cent of the cropped area. Barley was of local importance around Ormskirk, which had got a reputation for growing fine malting barley for the Midland breweries.[15] It has already been seen that there was a ready market for hay. Farmers aimed at get two cuts of hay from the grass in its first year and one in each of the following two years. The single most important crop, however, was potatoes, which filled 18.91 per cent of the total area under crops. In November and December 1878 1,000 tons each month were despatched from Rufford Station and it was claimed that 50 loads of potatoes daily arrived at Ormskirk.[16]

13

There was a tradition of potato cultivation from the early seventeenth century in Lancashire, with the early establishment of a potato market at Wigan. The origins of this tradition were supposed to have been the wreck of an Irish ship somewhere off what is now Southport and the arrival on shore of potatoes from its stores. Whatever the real origins, cultivation spread, and a thriving export trade had grown up by the mid-eighteenth century. The physical layout of farms, with small sheltered fields, coupled with a mild climate and deep moss soil, favoured its spread.[17] Both early and main crops were grown. The former were interplanted with cabbage between the rows, enabling two crops to be taken off the same land in a year. A wide variety of other crops was also grown, with patches of local specialisation. John Hampson, for example, grew on his Aughton Moss holding in 1858, besides the crops already mentioned, 15 butts of onions, three-quarters of an acre of carrots, "cellery several drills", cauliflowers, peas, turnips, broccoli and mangel wurzels. By the mid-nineteenth century the form of cultivation was intensive arable and the farmer's aim was "to sell everything his farm produces when it yields him a remunerative price, and to buy in return what is requisite to keep it in high condition".[18]

(b) Gentlemen and "peasants"

When one comes to look more closely at the character of those who farmed the south west the eye is drawn immediately to the large "progressive" farmers. Dickson pointed out "the considerable difficulty involved in delineating, with any tolerable degree of correctness, the character of so very mixed a class of men as that of the farmers of this county"; small and large farmers possessed "different views and different interests, with very different habits and notions". Even the best of small farmers, he argued, followed rigidly the habits and customs that had been handed down to them without any attempt to improve them. To large farmers, on the other hand, "the county is indebted for most of its improvements in husbandry, as well as much of that spirit of improved farming which is beginning to extend itself".[19] One such farmer who stands out, as he also stood out to Mingay and the mid-nineteenth century writers, as worthy of a closer look, is Robert Neilson.

Robert, and later his son (also Robert), farmed 300 acres at Halewood Green. This enormous farm, by the area's standards, grew the usual crops outlined above but also supported a dairy herd which was housed all year and fed on straw, turnips and oilcake. Large numbers of labourers were employed. Before mechanisation gangs of between 60 and 100 men were employed on weeding and harvesting. In lifting the turnip crop their efforts were aided by a light tramway readily moved across the field. More spectacular was the use of steam for ploughing. Neilsen's use of this began in 1863 when a 12-horsepower Fowler engine, together with four furrow plough and cultivator, was purchased at a cost of around £1,000. The farmstead housed a gas engine powering a threshing mill and equipment in the blacksmith's and wheelwright's shops. Neilson invented a system for drying hay in the stack, and was the first farmer in the county to use the

14

reaper and binder. All these exploits earned special praise from commentators as leading the cause of progressive agriculture.[20]

Neilson was an important figure at parish and county level. Starting his public service as a churchwarden in 1843, he became a J.P. four years later. He then became deputy lieutenant for the county and deputy chairman of the county Quarter Sessions under Derby, his landlord. In 1882 his daughter married the son of Samuel Graves who had been M.P. for Liverpool. Neilson's own politics were Liberal, although he was never particularly active. More important was his position as the first chairman of the Liverpool United Tramways and Omnibus Company.[21]

Yet behind this public success lay the fact that Neilson simply did not pay his rent. In 1872 he was only paying £400 out of a rent of £600 and had run up arrears of £10,000 – about half the value of the farm. By 1880 the arrears had risen to £15,000. The reason for his inability to pay, according to Derby, was a lack of capital, although he had other means besides the farm. The reason why he had been allowed to run up such arrears was harder to fathom, as Derby found. His agent Hale, he wrote, "seems for years to have acquiesed in his paying up as much or as little as he liked. There is something in the transaction which I have never understood". As he found, Hale seemed "uneasy if the subject is mentioned and continues to evade giving an answer". There was little that could be done with the arrears – "I do not wish to press him harshly, nor would that be politic".[22] It would certainly not be easy for the Chairman of Sessions to evict his deputy chairman, although other tenants would not be allowed to run up such arrears. The whole saga, however, illuminated the fact that the "progressive" farmers beloved of the agricultural writers were not necessarily practising methods appropriate to the conditions.[23]

The real key to success lay not in the use of machines that reflected the age's fascination with steam technology, but with the adoption of farming methods that were relevant to local conditions. Only in this way could farmers compete in the new markets. The crucial advantage that larger farmers enjoyed was the capital necessary to "play the market". Main crop potatoes, for example, were not sold immediately but rather were stored to be released on to the market when the price was right. Large farmers who had the ability to store potatoes through the winter would attempt to corner the market in the early spring. In 1914 one such attempt failed, as reported in the *Southport Visitor*:

> At the Ormskirk Farm Produce Market on Thursday it was reported that the attempt to "corner" the old Lancashire potatoes for chipping purposes had failed . . . the farmers who preferred not to sell the old potatoes when the demand was good have sustained heavy losses.[24]

Small farmers did not have the financial resources to attempt such a course and were forced to sell immediately to dealers, a matter for periodic complaint. In particular, the growing scale of the trade was such that farmers could not sell direct to consumers. The bulk of the crop went to the East Lancashire towns or, from Rufford, to London, Birmingham and Wolverhampton. Farmers argued that dealers had formed associations to protect their interests and farmers should do likewise, negotiating with the railways for waggons to send loads direct.[25] Nothing of this sort ensued, however, and farmers were left very much dependent on dealers. Indeed some dealers began to move directly into farming. James Martland, a potato merchant in Burscough Bridge, was already farming 125 acres when he applied to the Scarisbrick Trustees for a vacant farm "principally to grow potatoes upon for Seed purposes".[26]

A similar use of financial resources was applied to the sale of hay. Stacks of old hay in the yard "showed that the tenant had plenty of money to enable him to overhold his produce in anticipation of an advancing market".[27] Again, such farmers could afford to buy in sheep and cattle from the Welsh and Scottish hills. Pastured on the rich "aftermath" or "foggage" left after the hay harvest these fattened quickly for the Christmas market.[28] Access to finance to carry out these operations was limited. The major sources were farmers' own accumulations, and the family. Landlords were able to provide credit by postponing the collection of rent and very rarely might provide direct loans to tenants in trouble. In 1896, for example, the Speke estate made a loan of £400 to William Harrison of Blacklock Hall, although this did not prevent his eventual failure.[29] Farmers could get loans from money-lenders, but this was usually only a last resort. William Harrison included amongst his creditors the Union Loan Company. In the case of Sumner vs. Levy, in 1879, the plaintiff was a farmer in Halsall who had borrowed £88 from a Liverpool money-lender. Before going to him Sumner had taken out and repaid loans from, amongst others, the Everton Loan Company, the Albion Loan Company and the Liver Company. He became unable to continue his repayments and so borrowed a further £530 in cash with interest to pay of £37. His goods were seized before he could repay and he had to go to another money-lender to get a loan of £55.10s on a bill of sale at a rate of 25 per cent to get them back.[30] At such rates money-lenders were obviously a last refuge for the desperate. It was more usual for farmers to borrow money from relatives. Mary Blundell's father had "no money to start off with but he borrowed it off an uncle of mine you see, but he paid it back in under four years".[31]

The difficulty of access to finance, combined with market and environmental conditions, encouraged the growth of intensive vegetable production. Entry costs were low and the major requirement, labour, was readily available in the family. This gave a particular edge in labour intensive early potato growing. The extent to which small farmers did, however, continue to compete with their larger neighbours can be seen in the way in which new implements were adopted. One example of the way in which small farmers coped with the introduction of machinery is seen in the dominance of the combined reaping and mowing machine.[32] This was despite the technical difficulties involved in cutting the two crops:

> the corn crop was stiffer to cut than hay and could not be left lying loose on the ground . . . wide angled triangular knives with saw edges were found least liable to choke in grain crops, compared with the smooth edged, sharp-pointed knives that worked best on grass.[33]

These points have led one writer to claim with regard to reaping machines that

> it became necessary to divide the machines into three classes; side delivery, those without

16

side delivery, and combined reaper-grass mowers. The last combination was never perfected and mowing machines became a separate item.[34]

It seems that in south-west Lancashire farmers' ideas of what constituted "perfection" diverged considerably from those of engineers. Many small farmers were selling the same produce in the same markets as large farmers, and so were forced to adopt machinery in order to compete. However, the individual acreages of hay and grain crops would not justify the acquisition of two expensive machines. For example, John Pilkington of Burscough in 1868 grew on his 57 acres, 13 acres of wheat, 11 acres of oats and 13 acres of clover.[35] For such farmers the combined machine provided an economic alternative to separate mowers and reapers, even if it meant the sacrifice of a certain amount of technical efficiency. Demand for these machines was such that it supported a local manufacturer, Wilson of Tarleton. Another means of securing the advantages of machinery cheaply was to share the burden with other farmers. One machine for which this was particularly widespread was the winnowing machine, and examples turned up in sale notices of half or even third shares for sale. Other implements that were shared were rollers, corn drills and even ploughs.

It is difficult accurately to define a "small" farmer, as this depended on the type of crops grown; a 20-acre market garden, for example, was large. However some comparisons may be valuable. The average farm size in England in 1875 was 58.54 acres; in Lancashire it was 33.74. 80 per cent of the county's holdings were under 50 acres, as compared to the national figure of 71 per cent. The inadequate figures available for the south west indicate that 75 per cent of farms in the area were under 50 acres. Above that size it was almost certain that labour would have to be employed; in Tarleton in 1871 90 per cent of the 20 farms between 50 and 99 acres did so. Below 50 acres the proportion dropped to 46 per cent.[36]

The largest farms, those over 100 acres, were confined to those areas, such as Aintree and Speke, in the vicinity of Liverpool that had been under cultivation for many years, the home farms of the large estates, and the reclaimed areas like Marten Mere. Robert Neilson's farm was one of the latter category. The nature of settlement before large-scale reclamation had led to small farms and this continued as the dominant form into the twentieth century. It came under attack from some landlords. At Speke 25 farms averaging 84.5 acres had been reduced to 20, with an average size of 108 acres, by 1871.[37] This was on prime wheat growing land, however, and the same option was not open to other farmers. Some felt constrained by other factors to leave small farms alone. Derby visited some farms on Knowsley Moss and wrote regretfully that "these small holdings, 20 acres each, are liked by the tenants, but will never repay the money laid out upon them". His estate, however, contained fewer farms of this category than in the area generally. In 1895 44 per cent of his tenants farmed under 50 acres. The majority of holdings were under 75 acres.[38] Some agents were by contrast positively enthusiastic about small farms. They cost more in buildings, as the agent to the Scarisbrick Trustees recognised, but they paid "a third more rent than large ones". "The smaller the farms in this neighbourhood", he reported, "the greater the demand for them and the higher the rents . . . Besides this class of Farms is more easily worked by a family independently of paid labour, and are kept in a higher condition than larger holdings".[39]

This is not to say that landlords did not have a considerable struggle to force small farmers to change their ingrained habits. Their tendency was to farm as their fathers had done. One outdated practice that the Scarisbrick estate waged war on was moss burning. Tenants were allowed to burn the rushes and tough grass pared from uncultivated moss, but were strictly forbidden from doing so on reclaimed land. Nevertheless they persisted. The reasons given were two-fold. One was that the roads were so inadequate as to prevent them from manuring the land. The other was that tenants "were bound to manage their land according to the custom of the country and they therefore burnt because their neighbours burnt".[40] The estate was determined to stamp out a practice which meant that, as they told the tenants, "you are dissapating and making into cinders that which you ought to have increased in depth by deep plowing, and improved by Manure, Clay and Sand".[41] Accordingly those tenants who did not hold their land on leases were made to sign agreements not to burn. Those who still continued to burn were fined £2.

No such measures could be taken to improve the social character of tenants. These were working, not gentleman, farmers, a difference which displeased some landlords. Thus after a visit to Bickerstaffe in 1870 Derby noted that "there is much agricultural improvement and the farm buildings are mostly substantial and good, but the way of living of the farmers seems rough, and neither they nor their gardens are well cared for".[42] A return visit in 1886 found little improvement. He was introduced to a father and son partnership who "seemed well off, but the dirt & untidiness of the house & yard nearly turned my stomach . . . They are good tenants but live like pigs."[43] It was of such men that his agent wrote disparagingly that "There can be no reason why they should not join the Yeomanry if they like, but I doubt there being a horseman amongst them, or a horse suitable for a charger". The situation had evidently not improved since his report on the Knowsley tenants in 1863 when he wrote that "the condition (& habits) of the Tenants is not as satisfactory as I could wish".[44] To such people, as to other observers, there was little to distinguish farmers from their workers. As a newspaper report of 1879 commented, tenants "who are reputed to have accumulated modest fortunes from the farming of their holdings, could not be distinguished upon the day of our visit from any of their workmen".[45] Many small farmers had been employed before getting a farm of their own; others shared their farming with other occupations. In Aughton it was suggested that, with regard to the carting of road materials for the council, "arrangements could be made with a few of the smaller ones, who have not enough work on their own land to keep them occupied, for the carting to be divided among them".[46]

Another factor distancing small farmers from both their landlords and the gentlemen farmers was their adherence to Dissent. Particularly in the northern half of the plain, the Church of England could not "break down the strong Dissenting spirit".[47] Dissent was particularly strong in the northern half of the plain. This was an area of absentee landowners, with clergy who strongly identified with the rulers of rural society and with a concentration of small farmers.[48] A leading example of the appeal of nonconformity to the hard working independent small farmer was Edward Bridges, the "Hero of Rufford". According to his biographer

> he was not "slothful in business" while he was "fervent in spirit, serving the Lord". He knew also how, as the steward of God to make his business a means of grace; a secret which it behoves every Christian to discover, and then the more business the better for the soul. He was considered one of the best farmers in the neighbourhood.[49]

This pattern was broken in the areas fringing the Mersey where Roman Catholicism was dominant. It came under pressure from the influx of Irish migrant labourers with a very different version of faith to the essentially moderate creed of the gentry, but it was remarkably successful in cementing small farmers, farm workers and landlords. The Church of England could never match its success and remained the church of the landlord and the gentleman farmer.[50]

Farmers were not a homogeneous class. At one end of the spectrum were those (very few) on easy terms with their landlords, sharing in the administration of rural society. At the other end were the small holders who combined farming with other trades; at this end the distinctions were blurred, with farmers working alongside landless labourers. Many small farmers relied totally on family labour. Above this level were those farmers, employing labour, who formed the backbone of the staunch Dissenting tradition. What united all, however, was the dominance of the market. This was not an area of differentiation of farming systems according to size, as might happen in stock-rearing areas. In other parts of Lancashire, small hill farms reared stock which was fattened on large lowland farms. On the plain, by contrast, farming systems were virtually the same across the size spectrum, with the exception of market gardening at the bottom. The competition this entailed forced all farmers, for example, into the rapid adoption of machinery. There was thus a tension within the ranks of the farmers that was to display itself when the long golden age of prosperity received a jolt in the last decades of the century.

Notes
1. *J.B.D.F.A.*, X, 1895, p. 141.
2. "The Food Supply of Manchester", *J.R.A.S.E.*, 8, 1897, p. 207.
3. Central Reference Library, Manchester, First Annual Report of the Committee of the Manchester Farmers' Club, 1873, pp. 15-16.
4. *J.R.A.S.E.*, 8, 1897, pp. 208, 210, 212.
5. F. M. L. Thompson, "Nineteenth Century Horse Sense", *Economic History Review*, 29, 1976, p. 80.
6. *Journal of the Manchester, Liverpool and the North Lancashire Agricultural Society*, 1893, p. 136M.
7. F. Gray, *The Manchester Carriage and Tramway Company*, Rochdale, 1977, p. 89.
8. *J.R.A.S.E.*, 15, 1877, p. 486; Thompson, *op cit.*, p. 77. See also S. Heaton, 'The City Dray Horse', *J.R.A.S.E.*, 70, 1909, p. 63.
9. Manchester City Council, Proceedings, 1890-1, p. 1127.
10. 15 tons of manure a year: *J.R.A.S.E.*, 15, 1877, p. 486. Horses needed 1.4 tons of oats and 2.4 tons of hay per year: Thompson *op cit.*, p. 78.
11. J. Grundy, *op cit.*, p. 13; *J.R.A.S.E.*, 15, 1877, pp. 473, 486.
12. R. W. Dickson, *General View of the Agriculture of Lancashire*, London, 1815, pp. 230-1.

13. Samuel Lewis, *Topographical Dictionary of England*, London, 4 vols., 1849. The parishes were Aintree, Aughton, Bickerstaffe, Burscough, Lathom, Lydiate, Rufford, Scarisbrick and Tarleton.
14. These figures, and those which follow, are extracted from the manuscript Agricultural Returns in the Public Record Office, London.
15. *Orms. Adv.*, 2 October 1901; *Preston Herald*, 6 July 1901.
16. *Orms. Adv.*, 25 September, 2 October 1879; S. Jacquest, *Emmanuel: The Story of Methodism in the Ormskirk Area, 1792-1978*, Ormskirk, 1978, p. 44.
17. See R. N. Salaman, *History and Social Influence of the Potato*, Cambridge, 1949, pp. 453-4.
18. James Caird, *English Agriculture 1850-51*, London 1968, pp. 269-70.
19. Dickson, *op cit.*, 117.
20. *J.R.A.S.E.*, 1867, p. 392; 1882, pp. 650, 702; *J.M.L.A.S.*, 1872, p. 36; "Mechanics on the Farm", *Field*, 1882, 22 April, p. 545; William Garnett, "The Farming of Lancashire", *J.R.A.S.E.*, 1849, p. 392; J. Caird, *English Agriculture 1850-1*, London (1852) 1968, pp. 270-1.
21. James Eccles, *Centenary of Halewood Parish Church*, Liverpool, 1939, p. 24, 33, 34.
22. Derby diaries, 24 June 1872, 18 December 1880, 15 January 1882.
23. For further examples see Hale correspondence, 17 March 1871; *Orms Adv.*, 6 April 1871; *J.M.L.A.S.*, 1867, pp. 43-4; L.R.O., DX/1960, Handbill, "Agency for the sale of Agricultural machines and implements". P.R.O., BT/31/589, Liverpool Farming Company.
24. *Southport Visitor*, 27 June 1914.
25. *Orms Adv.*, 16 January, 10 July, 2 October 1874.
26. DDSc 79/1/59, 21 September 1896.
27. *Orms. Adv.*, 7 August 1879.
28. *J.R.A.S.E.*, 1877, p. 465.
29. Lv.R.O., Speke papers 920SPE, 10/7, 19 March 1896.
30. *Orms Adv.*, 24 June and 21 August 1879.
31. Interview. John and Mary Blundell. (Farmer, northern half of plain).
32. Sale notices show combined machines on almost 60% of farms, mowers on a mere 8%. A. Mutch, "The Mechanisation of the Harvest in South West Lancashire, 1850-1914", *Agricultural History Review*, 29, 1981.
33. C. S. Orwin and E. H. Whetham, *History of British Agriculture 1846-1914*, Newton Abbot, 1971, p. 111.
34. M. Partridge, *Farm Tools Through the Ages*, Reading, 1973, p. 130.
35. *J.M.L.A.S.*, 1868, p. 49.
36. Comparisons are from data in the Board of Agriculture's Agricultural Statistics for 1875. (PP 1875 c.1303 LXXIX). South west figures derived from manuscript returns in the P.R.O. Tarleton labour figures are from the census enumeration records.
37. A. Mutch, 'Paternalism and Class on the Speke Estate 1870-1914', in A. Charlesworth (ed.), *Rural Social Change and Conflicts since 1500*, Hull, 1982, p. 109.
38. Derby diaries, 19 August 1870; Royal Commission on Agricultural Depression, Minutes of Evidence, PP 1894, c. 7400, XVI, p. 53.
39. DDSc 127/18, papers relating to agricultural depression, 1896.
40. DDSc 79/1/33, W. H. Talbot to C. Scarisbrick, 19 July 1849.
41. *Ibid.*, handbill.
42. Derby diaries, 21 December 1870.
43. *Ibid*, 14 October 1870.
44. Hale correspondence, 26 April 1872, 4 May 1863.
45. *Orms. Adv.*, 7 August 1879.
46. *Ibid*, 23 January 1879.
47. A. Hewittson, *Our Country Churches and Chapels*, Preston, 1872, p. 230.
48. For one such parish, G. Earl, *A History of the Church and Parish of St. Michael and All Angels, Croston*, Croston, 1983.
49. J. A. MacDonald, *The Hero of Rufford*, London, 1896, p. 231.
50. These issues are discussed in much greater detail in Mutch, *Rural Society*, pp. 225-55.

20

3

The Landlords

(a) Rulers of rural society

Dissent may have been the religious watchword of the small farmer, but his devotion in all other spheres to his landlord was to the exasperation of urban observers. Hewittson spoke of the "all-absorbing and everlasting passion of theirs for Lord Derby and his agent".[1] This loyalty was amply declared in the fulsome memorials beloved of the Victorian tenantry. According to the tenants of the Scarisbrick estate the Count de Casteja

> made himself deservedly popular by his agreeable manners, and it was felt by all that they could not be wrong in looking forward to the son walking in the footsteps of a father known for his justice as a landlord and his kindness as a friend.[2]

The relationship was perceived by tenants not as a power one, but as one between straightdealing men. "I have no agreements with Lord Derby for my farms", declared James Martland, "and we neither of us wish for any".[3] This staunch individualism underwent some modification towards the end of the century. It meant, however, that landlords could not expect tenants to follow every move they made without question. Derby, recognising this constraint on his actions, was "of opinion that the influence of a landlord in Lancashire qua landlord and apart from his personal & political character is exaggerated".[4] Landlords were in a position to exert considerable influence over their tenantry, but there is undoubtedly truth in Derby's statement. The examples of tenants standing out against their masters' political leads occur when the landlord breaks with tradition. Departure from the Toryism which was tenant gospel and expected landlord practice was resisted, as we shall see later.

In general, however, there was continuing loyalty to the ruling families, a loyalty which stood in contrast to the increasing divide between landlord and tenant. In the eighteenth century Nicholas Blundell of Little Crosby joined in with villagers' celebrations of traditional holidays. Thomas Eccleston of Scarisbrick, with 24 tenants and a rental of some £600, could record in his diary for 1769 that "John Owen came to live with me as Plowman for seven pounds per annm".[5] These instances of social closeness disappeared with the drive to improve estates. This brought in its train lavish building projects which served to emphasise social distance. As Mark Girouard points out, country houses were symbols: "They were not originally, whatever they may be now, just large houses in the country in which rich people lived. Essentially they were power houses – the houses of a ruling class".[6] The early nineteenth century saw large scale rebuilding, but none with such spectacular results as at Scarisbrick, whose 150 feet high clock tower dominated the flat plain.[7]

These ostentatious buildings reflected the fabulous wealth enjoyed by the few who controlled the destiny of the area. Control was very real in that Lancashire, even more than the rest of the country, was a county of rented land. In 1890 about 95 per cent of the plain was rented land, as compared to a national figure of 84 per cent. In only one parish, Aughton, did the figure for land farmed by the owner came close to ten per cent.[8] This rented acreage was moreover in a very few hands. There were no less than four 'Great Estates' of over 10,000 acres in the area: Derby, Sefton, de Casteja and Weld-Blundell between them controlled over 70,000 acres. A further 36,000 acres was shared between seven owners.[9] The impact of this concentration of power was deflected. The settlement pattern of the area was typically scattered. In those villages clustered round the great houses – Knowsley, Speke, Little Crosby – life could be closely regulated. The physical environment was reshaped to meet the picturesque fancies of the day and attempts made to reshape the habits of the villagers likewise.[10] Much of the population was, however, because of its distribution, not susceptible to such control. In addition the landscape did not lend itself easily to the picturesque. Of Knowsley Derby complained in 1880 that "no planting or building will make it other than a dull place".[11] This lack of attractiveness in the countryside from which they drew so much income led to effective non-residence on the part of many owners. Some land was held by those with their main estates at a distance, such as Lilford, whose chief residence was at Oundle in Northamptonshire. The two Scarisbrick brothers, beneficiaries of a trust covering 6,000 acres, resided in Germany. Sefton, owner of the second largest estate, preferred life at Sefton House in London's Belgrave Square to that at Croxteth. The premier landowner, Derby, was of course deeply involved in national politics which prevented him taking the detailed lead that might otherwise have been expected. He was, in any case, not particularly enamoured of the countryside or many of his tenants. He left Knowsley in January 1871, "with no regret . . . at this time of year the county has little to interest or pleasure". Apart from shooting his activities on the estate were motivated by duty rather than by pleasure. On Good Friday he attended the local church "which I should not do elsewhere, but here a compliance with custom is expected from the chief person of the place".[12] We have already seen the disdain with which he regarded some of his tenants. However Derby had at least a keen sense of what was expected of him. He was scathing of the lack of involvement of fellow landlords who had no external commitments. Of Sefton he wrote that "work is not a part of his family traditions". He was a man of pleasure "whose main passion seems to have been shooting". Sir H. de Trafford "cares little, as I am told, eccept farming, hunting and shooting". Weld-Blundell "appears something of a scholar and artist, having cultivated tastes and literary knowledge, but has never come to the front in any public capacity". Of Hesketh of Rufford he observed that "his tastes were for sport, and latterly he drank hard".[13] Derby's low opinion of many of the area's landlords was shared by Nathanial Hawthorne, who observed a sitting of the local magistrates. They "lounged into the court more as a matter of amusement than anything else, and lounged out again, at their own pleasure; for these magisterial duties are part of the pastime of the country gentlemen of England".[14]

22

The consequence of the absence of landowners was to put considerable power in the hands of estate agents. Landlords might attempt to keep track of events by correspondence but few could exercise the sort of control over day-to-day affairs that Adelaide Watt had over Graves, her agent at Speke.[15] More often agents had considerable discretion in their actions. It has been seen how Derby's suspicions were aroused by his agent Hale's dealings with one of his tenants. He discovered in 1876 that Hale had bought land for £15,000. "This is going a little beyond his province", recorded Derby, "and I shall tell him in as little disagreeable a way as I can". His actions seem to have had little effect as later the same year he complained that "estate expenditure is still far too much, and I despair of reducing it while Hale continues in charge".[16] Similarly, John Betham, agent for the Scarisbrick Trustees, found himself having to justify spending £180 rebuilding a farm in which he and a Mr Bell had an interest without first seeking permission.[17]

The selection of agents was tailored to reflect the social importance of their position. The applications for the Fylde agency on the Derby estates reached 600. Derby's first comment was that "many are . . . quite unsatisfactory – solicitors, surveyors and the like". When interviews took place his comments make clear the main qualification for the job: "Mr Hussey, the first, was a rough & rustic personage, not quite enough of a gentlemen for the place: the second, a Mr Powle, satisfactory in looks & manner, but rather young". In the end a nephew of Archbishop Trench was selected, "best both in regard to manners and to his testimonials".[18] Once selected, agents tended to enjoy long occupation of their positions. Hale was at Knowsley for 46 years, Wyatt in charge of Croxteth for 29 and Graves controlled Speke for 36. These top positions were also well rewarded. Hale's salary in 1871 was £1,200, at a time when farm workers received under £50 a year.[19] This was commensurate with the immense social importance of the position.

The centrality of the agent was recognised by farmers' representatives, one of whom attacked the Sefton agent, Wyatt, as being "the arch intimidator, and who, rightly or wrongly, has the reputation of meddling with the business of other agents, and through them, of bringing his influence to bear upon tenant farmers with whom he has nothing to do directly".[20] It was Wyatt who presided over the meeting held in Preston in 1875 to discuss opposition to the Agricultural Holdings Bill. The call for this meeting was signed by George Hale, George Drewry (agent to the Duke of Devonshire at Holker), and Thomas Fair (agent to the Cliftons of Lytham).[21] Thus there was a small group of agents representing the largest estates who effectively decided the policy for landowners. This influence was also exercised in less visible ways. The correspondence between Hale and Derby, for example, reveals that many of Derby's pronouncements on agriculture were largely framed by the agent. Agents also sought each other's advice on prospective tenants. When Peter Swift applied for the tenancy of a Speke farm the first step was outlined by the owner. She was to "at once write to Mr Hale respecting Mr Swift – but should you happen to see the latter you would of course not say anything about Mr Hale having been written to". Three days later the agent was instructed to see Hale "and if all he says is satisfactory both as regards character, and being a Churchman as well as a Conservative, you had better accept Peter Swift as tenant".[32]

There has been some debate as to how far landlords were concerned with their tenants' political views. David Spring has argued, against O. R. Macgregor, that landowners were chiefly concerned with their tenants' farming ability, rarely troubling themselves as to their political leanings.[23] The experience in south west Lancashire indicates that a false dichotomy has been posed: landlords were interested in both. Certainly, in Speke farmers had to be Conservatives; workers were screened, but not as tightly. This is not to argue that landlords were forever coercing an unwilling tenantry. On the contrary, for the most part, farmers accepted the political and social eminence of their landlords as part of the natural order.

It has been seen that a combination of the settlement pattern of the area and the effective non-residence of many landowners meant that in practice the exercise of this eminence was not as constricting as in other parts of the country. Landowners did, however, possess other important buttresses to their position. One was the economic dependence that the presence of their households created. Not only did large numbers find employment in the house and on the estate, but local farmers benefited from supplying produce. This economic dependence and its consequent effect on attitudes was reinforced by the careful use of charity.

Besides a feeling of gratitude, this use of the carefully timed gift reinforced the feeling of dependence by its arbitrary nature. In Speke labourers received coal at Christmas. An increase in spending on the Lilford estates in 1881 was "owing to the sum paid for Army blankets distributed to the Poor on the estate last winter".[24] In Rufford, Sir T. G. Hesketh paid for medical attention to the poor, and Lady Hesketh supplemented the money collected by the Clothing Club.[25] On the Scarisbrick estate a farmer recalled

> In years gone by the late squire sent valuers over the potato crop, and afterwards returned the rent to his tenants: not because they were over-rented . . . I hope God will bind our landlords on both sides of us to their tenants.[26]

Such acts reflected both kindness and a sense of reponsibility, but they also helped to maintain the authority of the estate by their arbitrary nature, and so perpetuated the inequality which made such acts necessary. Hence the opposition to the compulsion of the Agricultural Holdings Bill, with its threat of the substitution of universally applicable rules enforced by law for the careful distribution of benevolence and the "regulation of . . . compensation by private agreement".[27] The combination of economic dependence and benevolence was successful for the most part in continuing the traditional loyalty of tenants to their landlords. There was however one issue which on occasion threatened the peace. This issue was game.

(b) Game: a double-edged weapon

Game was of central importance to the Victorian landowner. This can be seen in Nicholas Blundell's diary. Whilst he was a member of one of the leading

Roman Catholic families in the county, his diary contains few references to religion, save for the major festivals of Easter and Corpus Christi. The comparative lack of detail on religion is in sharp contrast to the careful recording of sporting matters.

In 1861 the year commenced with a shoot at Little Crosby which bagged 72 pheasants, 29 hares, 19 rabbits and 3 woodcock. Six further shoots followed in January and February, accounting for at least 327 birds and animals. By mid-February hunting with various packs of harriers makes an appearance. This took Blundell to Prestatyn, Altcar, Longton, Sefton, Aintree and Wrightington. There followed a lull until the beginning of grouse shooting, when he was away for seven days. Shooting began again in September and the year ended on an unfortunate note when he recorded, "I had the misfortune to shoot one of the beaters named Edwards the blacksmith in the leg in the shooting of a rabbit".[28]

Game in Lancashire meant shooting. The terrain was either too rough or too intensively worked to be hunted over, and those seeking fox hunting had to join either the Cheshire Hunt or travel to the Shires. (Lord Sefton, at the beginning of the century, was a legendary Master of the Quorn and played a large part in the development of that hunt and of hunting in general).[29] The figures recorded in Blundell's diary are insignificant compared to the slaughter that took place on other Lancashire estates. On the grouse moors of Abbeystead eight men shot 2,929 grouse on August 12th, 1915 – a world record.[30] In 1868 a "grand battue" with royalty in the party was held on the principal cover at Bickerstaffe on Derby's estate and 1,162 birds were killed, at that time "the largest quantity of game ever killed by six guns on any beat in Lancashire".[31]

The wider importance of game is perhaps illustrated by the fact that despite an absentee landlord who did not shoot, game was still carefully preserved on the Speke estate. The composition of the shooting party in 1895 is informative. The six guns, in addition to the Speke agent, included Colonel Ireland-Blackburne, landlord of the neighbouring Hale estate and Colonel Wyatt.[32] Clearly such shoots performed a useful cohering role in the ranks of the rural ruling class. The shoots at Knowsley reached far wider, covering local landowners, royalty and representatives of foreign governments.[33]

However, game carried more significance than this provision of a forum for an exchange of information. They were a form of ritual cementing the bonds of rural society. As one farmer put it, "Nineteen men out twenty round here are, I believe, quite willing to keep game for the landlord, and they like to see him shoot. It is a sympathetic tie between landlord and tenant".[34] In earlier leases this tie was institutionalised, as in the obligation on the Speke estate to "keep on the premises one game dog or bitch, and a cock in good condition, for the said RICHARD WATT, his heirs and assignees yearly, or when required".[35] There was an admiration of the sporting prowess of landlords. It is impossible to convey in print the feeling with which one farmer's son who loaded for shooters on the Scarisbrick estate remembers "They could shoot you know, aye they could".[36] This interest meant that the Bickerstaffe shoot was "always a redletter day amongst the Bickerstaffe tenantry", and on the shoot noted above "There was never such a crowd of spectators present before, and at times the line of beaters was a dozen deep".[37] The shoot offered a day off from routine, with the prospect of a good feed for beaters, a chance to admire the shooting skill of the landlord and his guests and, for the tenants, a present of game, "to let them share the spoils like". Derby was contemplating a reduction in the amount of game preserved in 1870 but, he wrote, "nor do the tenants complain, as game is liberally distributed among them".[38]

Game thus provided an interest which cut across class boundaries. But it was a double-edged weapon. Lancashire became well known as a county for complaints by farmers against the depredations of game on their crops. "It is not my province", stated the judge of the Liverpool prize farm competition in 1877, "to touch upon the game question, that being a matter of arrangement between landlord and tenant; but some of the fields suffered to some extent from their proximity to the game preserves".[39] Thanking his landlord for a rent reduction, William Cartwright of Speke complained,

> you do not appear to have taken into consideration the damage done to crops on my farm by game and it is very unpleasant to be always complaining about it, I would feel very grateful if you would allow a little more on that account.[40]

Feeling was particularly strong against those who rented shooting. The Earl of Sefton's agent reported that

> I have always heard a much stronger objection on the part of tenants to Keep the Game on Manors that are *let*, than where directly preserved by the owner, and this feeling prevails amongst your Lordship's tenantry.[41]

Before the Ground Game Act of 1882 tenants had no right to kill hares and rabbits feeding off their crops. The better estates would allow tenants to take ground game, but it was made very clear that this was a privilege, and a restricted one. In 1872 the Scarisbrick estate allowed its tenants to use traps and snares to take hares and rabbits; "All other modes than Traps and Snares are prohibited; neither Nets, Dogs or Guns are allowed". Further it was made clear that "The right of shooting (including every kind of Game) is exclusively reserved for the Marquis de Casteja and his Friends and authorised Gamekeepers".[42] Previous to this, it was alleged that a tenant of the estate was given notice to quit in 1858 despite being an improving farmer:

> And why? because my brother was found running after a hare, which was a mortal sin not to be pardoned. But he did not on the farm nor on the estate. My father was as innocent as the man on the moon, so was I, who was practically his farm bailiff expecting that as soon as father thought proper I should have the farm. I went to the hall to see if the place could be turned over to me. The answer I soon received was short and decisive – no![43]

Even after the act it was alleged that its provisions were widely flaunted and that, "in many cases if the tenant shot a rabbit he would get notice to quit at once". Evidence was given to the Royal Commission in 1894 of the instigator of a tenants' memorial asking for the implementation of the Act being given notice.[44] This accumulation of grievances meant that one of the attractions of Essex for Lancashire farmers who moved there was the absence of sporting landlords. In the districts they had come from,

26

Large quantities of game and rabbits were reared which damaged their crops, and the landlords were careless of their concerns in their shoots, trampling over their crops, and leaving gates open, etc. A frequent source of trouble and annoyance also came from the gamekeepers, who were forever suspecting and accusing them of keeping poaching dogs. The whole thing was a source of friction.[45]

Game also caused friction with labourers. Farmers had a measure of involvement. They might be asked to keep a dog, their sons might act as beaters, and they would often receive a gift of game after a shoot. Labourers shared no such involvement. They failed to join with landlords in equating poaching with theft and thus conflict, sometimes violent, ensued. In 1849 keepers in Altcar on the Sefton estate clashed with poachers with the result that "both parties are considerably injured by bludgeons, and seven out of a Gang of eight were captured". Two years later three poachers were apprehended; "White and his men acted very gallantly in the affair, giving the fellows a sound thrashing". In the following year 36 tame pheasants were stolen out of pens containing 76 birds, and three were found with their heads twisted off.[46] Later in the century such violence was rare and poaching seems to have become a much more solitary affair.[47]

Game played an ambiguous role in rural society. On the one hand it provided an interest which cut across class divisions. On the other it was an exclusive sport with strictly enforced rules and a body of keepers to ensure observation. The damage done to grain crops was an irritant in the otherwise smooth relations between farmer and landlord. Game also provoked a conflict between the laws of property and vaguer customary notions. Game was one issue which had the potential to bring landowners' authority into question. In general, however, they proved successful in having their leadership of rural society accepted as natural. This was achieved by a subtle mixture of economic power and benevolence. The aim was to create local communities with the estate at their centre, in which all had their place with its attendant rights and duties. The cement which held this together was charity, which was a measure of both the giver's benevolence and the recipients' dependence.

(c) Landlords and politics

The success of the landlords' policy in being leaders of local communities was clear in the extent to which tenants followed their lead in political affairs. However, opposition was forthcoming if this lead was at odds with tradition, and if any attempts were made to employ coercion. Landlords were not above using pressure to ensure that their wishes were complied with, particularly before the introduction of the secret ballot in 1872. Thus in 1844 the Earl of Sefton's agent is found reassuring his employer that;

> The tenants being qualified have been canvassed and your Lordship's wishes made known to them. I have every reason to believe that they will all vote for Mr Brown; tho' there are several (the Birches for instance) if uninfluenced would have supported Mr Entwistle.[48]

The most blatant case of pressure came in the 1868 election, when the major issue was the proposed disestablishment of the Church of Ireland. Gladstone and Greenfell, the Liberal candidates in South West Lancashire, were in favour of this, as was Anne, Lady Scarisbrick, who was a staunch Catholic.[49] She sent her steward round the tenants requesting them to sign a circular favourable to the Liberals. This persuasion to support a party "pledged to disestablish and disendow a church for which their forefathers shed blood" roused the anger of the *Ormskirk Advertiser*, but worse was to follow.[50] A local magistrate canvassed for the tenants' votes while his clerk recorded the decision and

> the steward looks steadily at the poor tenant who perhaps in some cases may be "a little in arrears for rent", in others "looking forward to assistance in the shape of drainage or other necessary farm improvements", or fearful of "going 'gainst t'new steward an' t'new agent".[51]

Representatives of the estate followed tenants to the ballot to ensure that they voted the right way. The case aroused so much feeling that Clifton of Lytham and other owners in the Fylde assured Scarisbrick tenants that if they were turned out for voting Conservative, they would attempt to find them new farms. During the election one tenant went so far as to purchase a farm in Burscough,

> for the purpose of lessening a bond, as he says "he means to vote as he likes" this time, which will *not* be for Gladstone and Greenfell whom Lady S. supports. The pressure in that quarter is so great that even Mr Wareing who has hitherto acted as Steward of the Manor to her Ladyship's satisfaction has been requested to send in all books & accounts of the Manor & has done so.[52]

Even after the Ballot Act accusations were made of threats by agents and in 1880 Tories found it necessary to place advertisements in the *Ormskirk Advertiser* reminding voters that "no one can find out how you voted" and carrying an assurance obtained from Lord Derby that "It is hardly necessary for him to say that he has never sanctioned and will never sanction, coercion or intimidation of voters in any form or for any purpose".[53] It was claimed that Lady Derby had accompanied a subagent canvassing for the tenants' votes for the Liberals: again this was a case of the landowner changing his traditional allegiance. At the time Derby wrote that

> Farmers and others who have not followed recent public events and who have always voted Conservative under the lead of my family, are puzzled by a change of front and I can't press them to go against what they may suppose to be their convictions.[54]

The tone of accounts by landlords of the use of their influence suggests a confident assumption that tenants should and would follow their wishes. In 1880, Nicholas Blundell of Little Crosby "went into the Village after breakfast with Sharman to see some of the farmers in reference to the approaching election, I having made up my mind to vote in favour of Blackburne & Cross the Conservative candidates" and later confidently recorded that "All my tenants and those from Ince went together to record their votes at Waterloo in favour of Blackburne & Cross in carriages and Omnibuses".[55]

This confidence was not misplaced. Landlords were Conservative by tradition and tenants followed this, returning Conservative M.P.s throughout our period. However, there were moments of opposition which fleetingly presaged the more serious threat to lordly authority that emerged in the last decade of the century. The first arose over the contentious issue of tithes, a sore point with both

Nonconformist and Catholic farmers. Some resistance to their collection was expressed in Croston, but outright refusal to pay did not emerge until 1884.[56] In that year John Williams, tenant of Black Moss Lane Farm, Burscough, withheld payment of £12 6s. 6d. and appealed for "active sympathy and support in my resistance to what is certainly a robbery of the farmers and workers for the maintenance of idlers".[57] His case was taken up by the newly formed Democratic Federation. Tenant farmers, argued its organ *Justice*, were looking to the land struggles in Ireland for an example. Democratic Federation literature had been widely distributed but farmers were too scared to complain openly for fear of losing their land. However, *Justice* claimed, "notwithstanding the silence there is under the surface, as I have had occasion to discover during my rambles in the neighbourhood, a deep and bitter class hatred".[58]

This was, in the event, wishful thinking. The Democratic Federation worked hard to win support, holding meetings in Burscough and Ormskirk. Williams successfully resisted the first attempt to distrain his goods and, reported *Justice*, "there is much excitement and the labourers and tenants are offering Mr Williams assistance and pecuniary aid". The movement spread to Scarisbrick and resolutions of support were forwarded from meetings held in Bristol, Blackburn and Birmingham. The second attempt to seize goods saw a crowd of between one and two hundred greet five police and four bailiffs. Copies of "socialistic literature" were circulated. The blowing of a horn brought seven Irish labourers armed with pikels and Williams with a revolver in his hand. However, the crowd gave at best passive support and the resistance fizzled out. Chairs were seized in lieu of the tithe, Williams was fined £50 for "riotously resisting" and the campaign collapsed.[59] It was not the end of John Williams' campaigning. In 1886 Derby was shown

> a socialist squib, the work of Williams and his friend at Ormskirk, which has more fun & less bad taste than such productions in general. It offers a reward for the discovery of two elderly men (Hale and Ward) who on Monday last took away the sum of £12000 in gold & notes being the property of farmers and others in the Burscough district.[60]

Despite Derby's apparent tolerance Williams was eventually evicted in 1888, although whether this was a direct consequence of his political ideas is not known.[61]

Williams met with a conspicuous lack of success, but a more serious challenge was launched by James Middlehurst. He took the tenancy of Berry House from the Scarisbrick Trustees in 1883. Unusually for a farm on the highly fertile black soil of the recently reclaimed Marten Mere he ran it primarily as a stock farm, breeding his own bulls and fattening bullocks in addition to a dairy enterprise. He embarked on a considerable programme of improvement on a run-down farm, estimating his expenditure over ten years at £2,237. He seems to have been an energetic and industrious tenant, and the *Ormskirk Advertiser* concluded in 1893 that *"no other farm* in Lancashire, or even England, can show such magnificent crops of oats".[62]

His energy extended to the writing of numerous letters to the *Advertiser*, mostly on the subject of foreign competition, the depressed state of British agriculture and the shortcomings of landowners. In 1889, for example, he was complaining about seeing unsheeted agricultural produce on a railway line, claiming that he had been told that sheets were to be forwarded to Liverpool. From this he concluded that foreign produce was being given unfair preference and that the remedy was for farmers to combine.[63] The aim of a farmers' organisation would be to obtain the reduction of rents and the abolition of controls on the free sale of land. The prospect awaiting farmers if they followed his advice was of a

> flood that, sweeping away all barriers, will emancipate our manacled farmers and give to them the same chances as their fellow men of reaping the results of industry, that is, the same chances of earning an honest livelihood for themselves and their families.[64]

To achieve this result farmers should be represented in Parliament by farmers, whatever their party allegiance. He put this argument into practice in the 1892 General Election. There was considerable dissatisfaction with the sitting Conservative member for South West Lancashire, R. B. Forwood, a Liverpool merchant and shipowner who had been Secretary at the Admiralty and, some felt, too far removed from the problems of local farmers. He had been returned unopposed at the previous election and Middlehurst called for a farming candidate to be put forward, stating that, if others joined him, he would be prepared to guarantee a salary and election expenses. No such candidate came forward and Middlehurst decided to stand himself. His candidature was endorsed by the Liberal Party, but he stood primarily as a tenant farmer. The major part of his manifesto dealt with his reason for standing:

> Because, after all the words I have heard from the lips of farmers respecting their great dissatisfaction with the late member, whom they regard as having nothing in common with them, and altogether unsuited to represent agriculture, and after the very many offers of votes I have received from farmers who have been Tories all their lives, I regard this as too good an opportunity to secure the representation of tenant farmers in Parliament by one of their own class to be thrown away.[65]

By contrast, Forwood's only mention of agriculture was to point to the late government's creation of a Department of State for Agriculture, concerning himself mainly with the need to maintain the union with Ireland.[66]

Middlehurst did not succeed in breaking down the traditional Tory allegiance of the constituency, but he did reduce Forwood's majority compared to the last time the seat had been contested. The turnout was low at 65.9 per cent, a figure attributed to the fine weather, as a result of which "both farmers and labourers were too busy amongst the hay to attend to the voting". This was important in a widespread constituency with large distances between polling stations and "any quantity of vehicles for Mr Forwood". Forwood secured 4,618 votes, Middlehurst 2,101, a majority of 2,517.[67]

These episodes show that not all farmers were prepared to accept their landlord's authority without question. They presaged in a small way the much greater strains put on landlord-tenant relations by the events of the 1890s. Before looking at them, we shall examine the impact of change on the farm worker.

Notes
1. Hewittson, *op cit.*, p. 378.
2. Souvenir of the homecoming to Scarisbrick Hall as Bride and Bridegroom of the Count and Countess Andre de Casteja, 1898.
3. DDSc 79/1/59, 24 December 1896.
4. H. J. Hanham, *Elections and Party Management: Politics in the time of Disraeli and Gladstone*, London, 1959, p. 288 citing Devonshire papers, 340.818.
5. DDSc 12733, 2 January 1769.
6. M. Girouard, *Life in the English Country House*, New Haven, 1978, p. 2.
7. P. Fleetwood-Hesketh, *Murray's Lancashire Architectural Guide*, London, 1955, passim. For Scarisbrick and its eccentric builder, see the fascinating account in M. Girouard, *The Victorian Country House*, Oxford, 1971, pp. 60-4.
8. Figures for south west and Aughton calculated from manuscript returns in P.R.O., MAF 68/1273.
9. Figures from J. Bateman, *The Great Landowners of Great Britain and Ireland*, 1883, Leicester, 1971. See also F. M. L. Thompson, *English Landed Society in the Nineteenth Century*, London, 1963.
10. See Mutch, *Class and Paternalism, op. cit.*
11. Derby diaries, 9 October 1880.
12. *Ibid.*, 31 January 1871, 15 April 1870.
13. *Ibid.*, 5 October 1887, 7 January 1874, 21 August 1872.
14. Hawthorne, *op cit.*, p. 444.
15. Mutch, *Class and Paternalism, op cit.*
16. Derby Diaries, 15 February, 18 July 1876. Cf. Thompson, *op cit.*, p. 178.
17. DDSc 79/1/57: letter to Sir Herbert Naylor Leyland.
18. Derby Diaries, 15 January, 22 February, 25 February, 11 March, 3 April 1886.
19. *Ibid.*, 9 January 1871.
20. *Orms. Adv.*, 2 November 1893.
21. L.R.O., Lilford papers, DDL 783 Box 5.
22. Speke papers, 13/6 17 October 1892, 10/6 25 October 1892. For further examples see Mutch, *Class and Paternalism, op. cit.*
23. D. Spring, *The English Landed Estate in the Nineteenth Century: its Administration*, Baltimore, 1963, p. 178.
24. DDL/78, steward's report, Bank Hall estate, 1881.
25. DDHe 104/7, Rufford Clothing Club; 104/9, Payment of medical expenses, 1859-66.
26. *Orms. Adv.*, 24 June 1880.
27. DDL 78/Box 5, Handbill. Meeting of land agents in Preston, 13 January 1875, to discuss the Agricultural Holdings Bill.
28. L.R.O., Blundell papers, DDBl 53/30, Diary of Nicholas Blundell, 1860, passim, particularly 8 January, 13 December.
29. D. Itzkowitz, *Peculiar Privilege; a Social History of English Fox-hunting 1753-1885*, Hassocks, 1977.
30. B. Hines, *The Gamekeeper*, Harmondsworth, 1979, p. 148.
31. *Orms. Adv.*, 16 January 1868.
32. Speke papers 13/9, 17 December 1895.
33. *Orms. Adv.*, 16 January 1868, 9 January 1879.
34. R. C. Agriculture (1895), Report, c. 7334, p. 47.
35. Speke papers 18/5, agreement with James Kerr.
36. Interview, John Blundell.
37. *Orms. Adv.*, 16 January 1868.
38. Derby Diaries, 8 December 1870.
39. *J.R.A.S.E.*, 1877, p. 471.
40. Speke papers, 18/12, 1 February 1886.
41. DDM 6/138, 10 July 1845.
42. Circular dated June 1872, in the possession of Mr E Rimmer, Bescar Lane Farm, Scarisbrick.
43. *Orms. Adv.*, 29 June 1893.
44. R. C. Agriculture (1894), Report, p. 49, Evidence QQ 14057-14064.
45. E. Lorrain Smith, *Go East for a Farm: a Study of Rural Migration*, Oxford, 1932, p. 34.
46. DDM 6/190 26 September 1849, 6/216 13 August 1851, 6/227 24 June 1852.
47. *Orms. Adv.*, 20 February, 27 February, 6 March 1879.
48. DDM 6/103, 24 May 1844.
49. For the background, see Hanham, *op. cit.*
50. *Orms Adv.*, 29 October 1868.

51. *Ibid.*, 5 November 1868.
52. Hale correspondence, 6 November 1868.
53. *Orms. Adv.*, 3 April 1880.
54. Devonshire papers, 340.999, cited in Hanham, *op cit.*, pp. 288-9.
55. DDB1 53/49a, Diary of Nicholas Blundell, 31 March, 6 April 1880.
56. Hewittson, *op cit.*, p. 188.
57. *Justice*, 31 May 1884.
58. *Ibid.*, 7 June 1884.
59. *Ibid.*, 7, 14, 21, 28 June; *Orms. Adv.*, 5, 12, 19 June; *Liverpool Review*, 8 August 1885.
60. Derby Diaries, 10 April 1886.
61. *Ibid.*, 6 May 1888.
62. *Orms. Adv.*, 13 July 1893.
63. *Ibid.*, 24 October 1889.
64. *Ibid.*, 20 March 1890.
65. *Ibid.*, 7 July 1892.
66. Ibid., 30 June 1892.
67. *Ibid.*, 14 July 1892.

Plate 2: Cottages at Formby, typical of those which accommodated the area's farm workers

4

Workers

(a) From servants to labourers

The immediate impact of "improvement" on the farm worker was the acceleration of the change from being a living-in farm servant, paid by the year, to a day labourer. At the beginning of the nineteenth century Dickson noted that "the large farmers commonly kept as many servants in their houses as are sufficient to perform the necessary business of the farms: but they begin to complain, in many cases, of the heaviness of the expense of this method, and more frequently employ day labourers".[1] The trend towards the employment of farm labourers rather than servants originated in the areas closest to Liverpool and gradually spread over the plain to the north. By the 1870s farm servants were in the minority across the whole plain. Writing in 1876 the Catholic priest of Lydiate stated that

> comparatively few young men are kept on farms, those that are engaged are chiefly "datal-workmen" (day-labourers), who are generally married men, and live elsewhere. This altered state of things is found to be advantageous to both parties, and is certainly much more conducive to morality.[2]

By 1913 an article in the *Ormskirk Advertiser* could bemoan the fact that there was little living-in compared to 20 or 30 years before, particularly in the Burscough, Rufford and Tarleton areas.[3]

There were two reasons for this change. One was the increasing desire of farmers to distance themselves from their labourers. William Rothwell recalled at mid-century that

> When I was a farmer, those servants who boarded in the house, partook at the same table as myself, and sat in the same room of an evening, talking over what we had done, how we might have done it better, and how we could best do the work tomorrow.

By 1850 however, "The great body of farmers seem to care little about their servants, except to extract the greatest amount of labour from them".[4]

The second reason was to be found in rising prices for agricultural produce and the total re-orientation of the market. The farmer preferred to sell all his produce for cash, paying his labourers in cash and letting them buy their own food, especially as "those who board with the farmer, live in a better style".[5] Wages also increased considerably, particularly after 1850, and this was a further incentive to cut down on labour.

A careful survey of agricultural wages in the county between 1812 and 1833 by J. D. Marshall indicates a growing uniformity of wage rates around the figure of 12 shillings a week. In areas such as Much Walton and Walton on the Hill, close to Liverpool, the rate was higher at 15s. a week. In Little Crosby in 1859 "a man of the agricultural class . . . considered himself well paid and a big wage if he got ten or twelve shillings for his week's wage".[6] Indoor servants, according to this writer, were paid £14 a year, whilst in Bickerstaffe in 1857 the rate was £12. The absence of a hiring fair, with the consequent publishing of wage rates in local papers, means a lack of evidence of movement of servants' wages. Labourer's wages, however, rose considerably to stand at at least 16 shillings a week by 1870. In 1877 earnings for labourers were estimated at 21 shillings, with servants receiving between nine and ten shillings, or a yearly rate of between £23 and £26. Lancashire farmers were at this time much agitated by the "Labour Question", but George Hale felt there was little they could do about it. He could not see

> how the labour question is to be met except by paying a market price for it – or when practicable doing without it. The wages around this place have risen considerably & are *paid* Farmers giving 16/- or 18/- to Labourers and £1 to teamsmen.[7]

With wages having risen by between a third and a half, there was ample incentive for farmers to reduce their workforce. One obstacle which stood in the way of their cutting down on the number of servants was the lack of adequate cottages for labourers to live in.

In the 1850s there was general condemnation of the shortage of housing for labourers and the unsatisfactory condition of what was available. In some districts, particularly around Warrington, "so great is the desire of some large proprietors to *avoid poor's rate*, that many cottages have either been taken down, or allowed to get out of repair until they fall".[8] Where there were cottages they were often far from satisfactory. Rothwell complained that

> There is often plenty of room, on the ground floor, but ill contrived, inconvenient, and too low overhead. In erecting them, comfort, which would have cost little more, has never been studied at all. The windows are small, often without casements, and the doors as misplaced as possible for affording warmth, or for providing sufficient and proper ventilation. The sleeping rooms are still more objectionable, the roof often coming down to the flooring, more like hen cotes, or pigeon boxes, than sleeping appartments for human beings: and of that class by which our very existence is at stake.[9]

By the 1870s farmers were complaining about their landlords' failure to provide cottages. Hale told Derby in 1872 that "the accommodation for Labour on or near a farm has been felt & is in the minds of Farmers as a necessity and has no doubt been much felt in many localities".[10] James Middlehurst complained that "To be able to keep men at Berry House, worth having convenient residences must be found . . . When they live three miles away it is most inconvenient for them".[11]

There was some building of cottages but it was very limited in extent. Landlords were still pulling them down and not replacing them. On the Lilford estates in 1875 the agent reported that "It is intended to pull down an old mud cottage entirely past repair at Bretherton, and I do not propose to rebuild it, cottages not being wanted there".[12] Some landlords, of course, provided good cottage accommodation. When Sir Thomas Hesketh inherited the Rufford estate, "on which, for a long time, under a previous regime, very little had been done", he

34

commenced a programme of improvement which included the building of "good semi-detached cottages standing in ample gardens".[13] In general, however, cottage provision was patchy and the decline in farm servants cannot be attributed to any significant increase in their numbers. Another reason must be sought for the farmers' ability to cut down on their numbers.

The opportunity was provided by the introduction of machinery. By 1871 around 40 per cent of farmers possessed some mechanical means of harvesting their hay crops, and around 20 per cent had machinery for corn cutting, proportions which were steadily increasing through the following decade.[14] This led to a reduction in labour employed. As T. E. Gibson observed, "the general introduction of machinery for farm purposes had led the farmers to employ a much less number of hands than they formerly did".[15] Not requiring so much labour, farmers could dispense with expensive living-in servants and rely on those who already had cottages. This is indicated by the changes in the numbers of workers in Aughton in 1871. The number of servants had dropped by 44.34 per cent, while the number of labourers had risen only by 28.47 per cent.[16]

(b) Work and wages

Those who remained to work the land were well paid by comparison with workers in other parts of England. In 1892, for example, average earnings in Lancashire were 19s. 8d. a week, as compared to 15s. in Norfolk, 15s. 6d. in Essex and 14s. 9d. in Wiltshire.[17] Wilson-Fox reported an average rate during the 1890s of 18 to 20 shillings a week in West Lancashire and 16 to 18 in Sefton. By 1903 wages in Sefton had come up to those in West Lancashire at 18 to 20 shillings, where they remained until raised by the strike of 1913. This level of pay was largely due to the ready availability of alternative work. Employment was available on the large-scale drainage schemes or on the expanding railway network. The latter also gave easy access to high-paid labouring jobs in the towns, as the Speke agent found to his cost in 1897 when he reported that "John Henry has left Speke and gone to live in Rotherham, he has gone to some Gas Works and is getting 40s. a week. I was sorry to lose him but I could not offer him anything like the wages he is getting there".[18]

"Outdoor" labourers fell into two categories, the "teamsmen" and the "datallers". Teamsmen were those employed on a regular basis throughout the year, the men who did the ploughing and the carting of produce to market. Datallers were day labourers, employed on a semi-permanent basis, frequently on piece work, on such tasks as weeding and setting potatoes, as well as the more skilled jobs such as hedging. If one compares a diagram of the wages expenditure on Mount Pleasant Farm, Speke, with one drawn from the Tewkesbury area it is evident that the seasonal labour demand was considerably different (see overleaf).[19] In the corn growing regions a furious peak of activity came with the harvest. South-west Lancashire had three harvests: hay in July, grain in September, and potatoes in October. There was plenty of work outside these

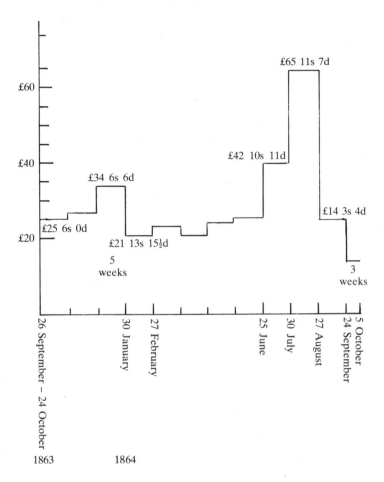

The year's wages on a Tewkesbury farm. *Source:* D. Morgan, "The place of harvesters in nineteenth century village life", in R. Samuel (ed.), *Village Life and Labour*, London, 1975.

periods of peak demand. Many farmers also grew early potatoes, and all were particularly busy during early spring seedtime.

At Speke, three men worked throughout the year. They were engaged during the winter months in ditching, in carting hay and potatoes to market, and in spreading the manure that came back as a return load. The onset of spring with ploughing and sowing led to the taking on of extra local men. Four such men were employed at Mount Pleasant on a fairly regular basis. At the times of peak demand, casual workers, usually Irish migrant labourers, but sometimes women, were employed. The regular men were on a steady weekly wage of 20 shillings a week in 1891; the other locals on 18 shillings. The casuals were paid by the

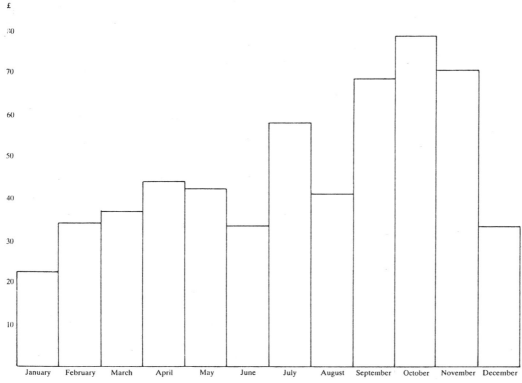

£

80

70

60

50

40

30

20

10

January February March April May June July August September October November December

Wages on Mount Pleasant Farm, Speke, 1891. *Source:* Wages Book, 920SPE 7/1

day or, as when lifting potatoes, on piece rates. A harvest bonus of 6d. a day was paid, together with drink.[20] The question of drink at harvest was a contentious one, and a concerted effort was made in Halsall in 1884 to end the practice. One farmer reported that, "they had not only managed to get in their harvest without beer last year but that there was nothing like the same amount of squabbling among the men as when there was beer".[21] The end of the nineteenth century saw a gradual substitution of money for beer.

These accounts confirm David Morgan's description of the "crowded fields" of harvest time, but in addition the fields of south-west Lancashire were crowded throughout the year. The cultivation of vegetables required constant weeding, particularly as the enormous fertility of the soil encouraged large yields of weeds as well as produce. In 1849, for example, Robert Neilson of Halewood employed "a large number of men in gangs of from 60 to 100, in hoeing, cleaning and reaping, so as to get through the work rapidly".[22] During the reclamation of a field at Berry House Farm which had been covered in twitch and wild mint "a big crop of thistles came and 22 men were kept hard at work getting this up".[23] When a party of Mersey farmers visited Hesketh Bank they were shown a ten-acre field of carrots which "it was said there had been as many as forty weeders in the field at one time".[24] The introduction of machinery diminished this demand for labour. The important machines were the self-binder for harvesting corn and the potato digger which arrived in the 1880s and 1890s respectively. Their main impact was on casual labour, whose weight in the agrarian economy is discussed below.

Working hours varied considerably according to the season. In the height of the hay harvest at Speke the agent reported that "I start the mowing machine at 6 o'clock in the morning & keep it going until 7 o'clock in the evening with two sets of horses".[25] One farm worker, who started work in the early 1920s, recalls that,

> I've heard them talk, the old farm workers, about going out into the field first thing in the morning and then when it went dark they used to get four pikels and a lantern at the end of each pikel and stick them in the wagon and then they kept on loading and they kept on to midnight, many a time it was midnight and then they went out again next morning at 6 o'clock.[26]

Part of the teamsman's job was to take produce to market. To walk to Liverpool with the horse and wagon would take two or three hours, which meant the teamsman setting out at three or four o'clock in the morning to be at the market for six o'clock.[27] They often had a considerable degree of responsibility for marketing the produce. When informing an applicant for the job of teamsman of his conditions of work the Speke agent stated that he would join his brother with responsibility for marketing. This arrangement was not always successful as in 1902 the agent complained "I can make nothing of Sumner as a market man".[28] Farmers resented the autonomy that this situation gave to their teamsmen and the opportunity which it gave for engaging in dealing themselves by giving dealers short measure for the farmer and selling the rest themselves — a practice which one farmer estimated cost him up to five per cent of the produce's value.[29] This autonomy was limited and the description by one teamsman of his job as "mostly work and bed, work and bed, and bein' out in all sorts o'weather, summer and winter" rings true. This teamsman went on to explain that

> There's most places where a horseman's expected to have his horses out by six in the mornin', and then happen he has to come to the station at night wi' tatoes. I've seen mysel' when I've given over in t'field at half past four in th'afternoon and then had to come t'station here wi' a load of tatoes and unload 'em; and then I've four more mile to go when I've unloaded 'em. And then, by the time as I've got th'horses in its been nine o'clock. And nothin' extra for it.[30]

38

(c) The Irish labourers

These were the conditions for local labourers, but an equally vital part of the workforce were casual migrant labourers. Agriculture's labour demand is seasonal. Before the introduction of machinery the need was for a large workforce at times of peak demand which could be dismissed as soon as possible when no longer required. One possible solution was that adopted in the south of England, with masses of labourers crowded into insanitary "open" villages, scratching a living through the winter on piecework hedging and ditching. Their only chance of high earnings came at harvest time. In Lancashire by contrast, the solution was to maintain a small, all-year-round workforce and rely on external help at times of peak labour demand.

At the beginning of the nineteenth century this demand seems to have been met by local people and there was a dialect word "quock", which meant "to go harvesting from home".[31] Handloom weaving was also an important source of harvest labour, but the growth of factories with their rigid discipline stopped up this source as "the manufacturing population cannot leave their employment on account of the machinery, which would have to stop. Forty years ago they could leave their looms, spinning jennies, etc., at any season for a few weeks".[32] While there were still several handloom weavers in Aughton as late as 1851, such sources were neither dependable nor adequate and by that time, "were it not for the Irish, the farmers could not get their work done in the busy seasons".[33]

The annual migration left physical evidence in the shape of the "Irishmen's house" or "shant" which were built on many farms. On a 181-acre farm in Aintree "nearly all" the labourers were Irish and lived in a "barracks", while on the 218 acre Edge Farm, Sefton, in 1871 the Irishmen's house was occupied by 14 Irishmen.[34] Such accommodation was generally very basic:

> they used to live in what they called a shant, which was an old brick one storey building, sometimes there was two stories and there was nothing in it. There was a fire, there might have been a cold water tap but more or less it was just a pump in the farmyard and they used to put chaff in bags for the beds, they didn't have any beds or anything, they used to lie on the floor in these chaff bags, very, very primitive it was.[35]

When Sutton Grange on the Speke estate was being improved in 1896 the agent reported that "You will remember what I said about the Irishmen's house being in such a filthy condition, that it necessitated the pulling down of these buildings".[36] Many farms did not run to the provision of special accommodation, however basic. At Barrow Nook, Bickerstaffe, the "Irish labourers have to sleep in a loft over the pig styes. The loft is divided into three compartments, or little rooms, one over each pig stye".[37]

Around 60,000 Irish migrant workers entered Britain in the 1840s, a figure which declined to 38,000 by 1880 and continued to decline, despite a slight upturn at the beginning of the twentieth century, to stand at 13,000 in 1914.[38] These crude figures do not distinguish which parts of Britain received the most migrants, nor the pattern of their internal migration once in Britain. Collins argues that there was a shift over time with an increasing number staying in the north and west. Many of these workers were also staying in the same area, although there was a northern England "circuit": Cheshire/Lancashire (hay harvest); Derbyshire/Shropshire/north Nottinghamshire (late hay harvest; early corn harvest); the Fens/Lincolnshire/Yorkshire/Staffordshire/Warwickshire (corn harvest); Cheshire/Lancashire (potato harvest).[39] While Lancashire might, compared to other parts of England, have a higher proportion of Irish harvesters, local commentators were very conscious of a downward trend in numbers. As early as 1857 there were warnings of a future shortage of Irish labour and by the late 1890s, "Irish harvesters . . . were hardly ever known to be so scarce".[40]

Irish labourers came to England because they had no choice. There was no question of their earnings being a valuable extra, for the Irish agrarian system forced them to find external employment. The small farmer would have to leave his holding in the care of his wife or he would send his children across. The grim necessity of migration comes across clearly in this description of a holding in Lecanry, Country Mayo:

> Man, wife, six children. Eldest son, 17; eldest girl, 16. Cottage; Rubble, stone and thatch. Living room 12×14, Bedroom 12×8. Holding 1 acre. Rent £2 10s. Husband goes to work in England. Last year was near Blackburn and made £4 clear, but he had a very bad season. He has often made more than that. He says: "If it was not for England we could not live at all".[41]

Wages varied from area to area and according to the type of crop. In Scarisbrick payment was per score yard for potatoes;

> By gum, they could get spuds! I remember a penny farthing a score for main crop, but if it was earlies they'd perhaps you see they used to inter-plant the earlies wi' greens, you know, cabbages on rucks . . . they used to have to put their tops in between and not bury cabbage, put the tops in between, put a bit of soil on and they'd get another hapenny a score for that you know.[42]

Around Garstang they could expect to get 24 shillings a week during the harvest and anything between 15 and 24 shillings for ordinary farm work. Lifting potatoes on piecework they could make up to 35 shillings a week. After deducting travelling expenses, it was estimated that if they stayed for several months, working regularly and living frugally, they could clear between £13 10s. and £17. As a rule they would be expected to find their own food, and their diet was usually a meagre one.[43]

Conflict between local and Irish labourers fell into two types: those caused by concern over jobs, and those with racial overtones. The first were rare, as the Irish were not usually in direct competition for jobs. One such conflict occurred during the 1842 strikes when the *Manchester Guardian* reported of Irish labourers that, "few of them found employment having been opposed in many districts by the English labourers including not a few who had been thrown out of work by the turnouts and the disturbance in the manufacturing districts".[44] This was obviously an unusual case, although discontent might be caused by the high wages which could be earned on piece work; "the irony of it was that the Lancashire farm workers used to set the potatoes and they used to, the farmers used to have Irishmen coming over getting them and they used to get more for getting them".[45]

The other sort of conflict seems to have been motivated by racial, political or religious hostility. In 1894 a number of Irish labourers were asleep in the "Irish" house on a farm in Altcar when "at about midnight the place was broken into and nine or ten entered and assaulted them . . . Sticks, pokers and other weapons were used upon the inmates". Five men were subsequently convicted on charges of arson, unlawful wounding, riotous assembly and wilful damage to property, and received sentences ranging from six months to five years.[46] The cause of the attack was not specified. There may have been antagonism either because of the area's tradition of popular Protestantism, or because of political struggles in Ireland. It has been seen that John Williams was supported by Irish labourers in his resistance to tithe collection. Another reason may have been that the Irish in the plain, as opposed to in other parts of the county, tended to work in large gangs. In 1887, for example,

> About 200 Irish harvesters principally belonging to the Mayo militia arrived in Ormskirk at midnight, and at the word of command they formed in procession, and marched through the streets in military order, armed with sickles, which they brandished in all directions, making the most hideous noises and breathing out threatenings of slaughter against the "hated Saxons". Having had possession of the streets in this way for about three hours the fellows were dismissed without any serious breach of the peace, but not without having caused considerable excitement in the town.[47]

Despite the panic caused by such incidents, they were not common. Most Irish labourers were too concerned with the grim economic necessity of making their visit profitable to get into confrontations. The need to make money made the Irish outwardly at least submissive and hardworking.

In a way women performed a similar function to the Irish, in being a source of seasonal labour. Indeed, as the century wore on they came to supplement the diminishing number of Irish potato harvesters. The position at mid-century was that a considerable number of women worked in the fields. As Barnes recalled of the late 1850s, "it was part and parcel of their engagements to assist in the season of setting potatoes, in the hay field and also in the harvest fields from early morning to as long as the men worked at night".[48] In 1856 Nathaniel Hawthorne noted near Southport that "people were harvesting their carrots and other root crops, and women as well as men were at work, especially digging potatoes".[49] It has been seen that at Rufford in 1871 women were employed planting potatoes and spreading dung. In 1881 Jane Howard, Jane Prescott and Alice Thompson were all binding during the harvest at Scarisbrick. They were paid 2 shillings a day; the men 3s. 4d. A similar inequality applied to the women who worked on Charles Allen's threshing team at Mount Pleasant, Speke, in 1892. Three of them received 2s. 6d. a day, while the men were paid 3s. 6d.[50]

The introduction of the potato digger brought new work for women, picking up the potatoes it unearthed and replacing Irish labour. In Speke the agent observed that "On account of the wet weather I have been unable to use the Potato digger and the men have been digging by the piece, but I now have a large staff of women as well as men, picking up after the digger". As the women were only paid 2 shillings a day it is not surprising that the saving made by using the digger was estimated at £20.[51]

(d) Getting by

The extent to which women worked in the fields, given the lack of evidence, can only be guessed at. The glimpses allowed show that their work continued throughout the period, even if the form changed. Similarly, it is not easy to gain access to their major role, of managing the family economy. Lancashire might have been a well paid region compared to the grinding poverty of other rural parts of England, but the possibility of real want was always present. This was graphically demonstrated by an appeal to Lord Derby in 1883, concerning the wife of Charles Knowles, a carter earning 18 shillings a week. His two boys were caught stealing from men servants at Knowsley Hall. One was sent abroad, the other to a school in London, for which Knowles had to pay five shillings a week. The letter begged for help, explaining that Ann Knowles could not pay the rent, for

> out of 12s. 6d. a week when her fire candles and club are paid she as little over 2d. each there is 4 – 1 a man turning out at 5 o'clock in a morning he must have meat to be able to follow his work the children to but it is telling upon her very much and as rent day draws near I see a great difference what she is thinking of doing I dont know as she makes no complaints it would be a deed of charity to give her one years rent which is £4 she is deserving of it she should not want rent nor taxes if I had it but I am onely a poor dependent I dare not give my name for fear I have given offence with begging for her it as been a sore trial for her trusting to Gods will and your lordships charity I am A poor Woman.

The agent's reply, a man whose weekly income was at least twenty times that of Knowles, is instructive of upper class attitudes towards poverty. He put the blame firmly on the wife's bad management, claiming that "The most respectable family in the Parish twelve in number were brought up – and were always tidy – on 12/- a week! So much for a thrifty wife".[52] A family with grown up children bringing money in would enjoy a higher standard of living but before then life could be a struggle. As Mrs Winstanley explained, "Ah've been fair moithered many a time to make do on your father's wage . . . afore Jack and Jim started to earn".[53]

Circumstances beyond the family's control could bring about hardship. Bad weather was a constant threat to those without permanent employment, particularly at the beginning of the period. Thomas Eccleston recorded in 1783 that, on account of a bad season, "the poor were much distressed, but a subscription was opened".[54] Blankets were distributed to the poor on the Lilford estates in 1881, and in 1879 two Croston farmers were congratulated for each giving a cartload of potatoes to the poor of the village. If others would follow their example, opined the *Ormskirk Advertiser*, "there is no doubt that the hunger and starvation at present so largely prevailing would be considerably alleviated".[55] Even in the estate villages want was present. Derby rather coldly

42

recorded in 1870 that, according to the vicar, "there is no destitution in Knowsley, and but little distress".[56]

Charity was one way in which such suffering was alleviated. This could either be by direct gift, as discussed above, or by the subsidisation of schemes designed to allow the poor a measure of "self help". One such was the store run on "the no credit principle" at Knowsley. Another was the clothing club. Into these concerns regular savings were made by cottagers and a bonus added by the landlord to the annual distribution. The Rufford Clothing Club had in 1845 38 male and 15 female contributors paying in amounts of 4d., 6d. or 1s. a month. Lady Hesketh subscribed £10, a Mrs Polk £2 and other benefactors £7, giving a total of £30 18s. for distribution. From this purchases of sheets, fustian, linen, shoes and a coat and waistcoat were made.[57] Thirty years later Hewittson found

> in Tarleton there are clothing clubs for the benefit of the cottage tenantry of both lords of the manor. These clubs annually produce £90 on the average, when the bonus is added, thus affording to the good housewives at the close of the year a welcome aid towards useful clothing of their own choice and purchase, for either themselves or their little ones.[58]

A more independent means of providing against the vagaries of rural life were the sick clubs. (The names chosen however, such as Lord Viscount Molyneux lodge of the Oddfellows and Countess of Sefton lodge of the Druids in West Derby, were indicative of continuing deferential attitudes.) The report of the Registrar of Friendly Societies for 1867 has returns from 54 clubs in south west Lancashire, 22 of which were local societies.[59] The gradual replacement of local clubs by lodges of national societies was a feature of the period. In Knowsley, for example, "The old sick club was dissolved some six or seven years ago, and many of the members joined the Oddfellows".[60] The 54 clubs had 6,210 members, a substantial proportion of the working population.

At the beginning of August each club held its annual club day. This commenced with a procession behind a local band from the club's meeting place to the church. After a service the members marched back for dinner and entertainment. Much to the disapproval of local worthies many club days ended in drunkenness. Thomas Barnes in 1910 looked back on club days in Little Crosby and recalled

> It was a great day in olden times for boath Old and young . . . There was one thing noteable on this day, or I may say in the evening there was shore to be a fight as the two township people were like to Clans, one against another, which had the best men. It was almost always settled with a fight each year, there was one Club Day in particular when there was four or five fights going on at the same time.[61]

By 1879 the *Ormskirk Advertiser* was welcoming the fact that "Club anniversaries have now taken the form of genuine enjoyment, harmless sport, and substantial festivity than formerly".[62] However it returned to a more censorious tone in 1884, complaining that "From an early hour in the morning, until late in the evening, women as well as men were seen in various stages of drunkenness". The problem was, argued the paper, that meetings were held in public houses. Worse, "On the annual day after dinner women are admitted into some of these rooms, and without any sense of shame drink along with the men".[63] The following year the *Liverpool Review* joined the attack, reporting that "In nearly every village the proceedings of 'Club Day' terminate with a carouse, and many members only reach home by the aid of friends".[64]

The tone of these comments reflects the constant attempts to reform labourers' habits, particularly their attraction to drink. Such attempts had more chance of success in villages under sole ownership. On the Sefton estates public houses were removed "where not absolutely necessary". By 1894 "the four public houses which, until a somewhat recent period, existed in Altcar are now no more, much to the moral benefit of the parish".[65] In other places such control could not be exercised. In Bretherton in 1872 it was said that "As at Tarleton, so here – ale and hard work are amongst the local deities".[66] In Tarleton in 1868, the *Advertiser* reported with disdain, "Three 'knights of the taproom' being rather short of cash (as such like often are) engaged for a small quantity of beer to strip off their clothes, all but their shirts, and in that state walked through the village". (All three were said to be married men in their 40s).[67]

A more successful attack was made on customary practices. In the 1840s an allowance of ale was made to singers when Altcar churchwardens were admitted to office. In the same parish on 'Braggot Sunday' in mid-Lent employers were expected to give eggs to their labourers, who drank them in hot spiced ale. These same labourers spent the Monday after 'Rushbearing Sunday' in heavy drinking. The first to fall asleep as a result was the 'mayor elect'. On the following day,

> dressed in an old hat and old clothes, with face blackened, the mayor was accompanied round the parish by neighbours, who danced round him to fiddle and tambourine and anything that would jingle and offered him various indignities. They wore extravagant garments, decorated with ribbons, and calling at various houses they passed, received money or drink.[68]

All these customs had vanished a few years later. Other customs survived with changed meaning. On Good Friday 1767 Thomas Eccleston had "200 people a begging for Peace eggs". By 1789 a halfpenny each was substituted for eggs.[69] The custom was restricted to children by 1867 and a ritual which had emphasised the customary obligations of the ruling class had become a children's entertainment.[70] In Aughton in 1893 boys decorated with ribbons and led by one of their number called "Tosspot", carrying a basket in which to collect eggs or money, performed a play with wooden swords in which one was wounded and called for a doctor who cured him. Eggs obtained in this way were hard boiled and stained with vegetable juices, and rolled in the field.[71] The passing of these customs reflected the end of a society based on customary obligation. Landowners sought to remould the behaviour of labourers to fit new ideas of respectability.

In line with these new ideas, other habits came under attack. Stanley recorded in his notebook for 1857 a conversation with the vicar of Bickerstaffe "on the state of the peasantry in these parts". He was told

> that a wedding to which the bride comes as a maid is the exception and not the rule: the common custom being, that the parties marry in time to avoid the reproach of an illegitimate child being born. He preached against their laxity in this respect and his sermon provoked quite as much surprise as anger. He said that the confidence of the parties in each other was very seldom betrayed; desertion after intercourse being rare, and held disgraceful on the part of the man.[72]

44

Whether there was any resistance or objection to the changes that happened to the working class in the middle years of the nineteenth century is a matter of conjecture. There was certainly no echo of the "Swing" riots that shook southern England in 1830. The popularity of fundamental Protestantism could be seen as one response to changes in wider society. Its heyday certainly coincided with the time of greatest change, the 1840s, the decade that marked the irreversible shift in the nature of the rural economy. A further safety valve was the easy availability of alternative work in the nearby towns. The vicar of Knowsley reported no discontent amongst the labourers there in 1872, at a time when much of southern and eastern England was seeing the birth of agricultural trade unionism. He did, however, add that the "disturbing agency in the minds of the working class hereabouts is Reynold's newspaper: they club to buy it: one reads it to the rest, and the writer's opinions are discussed".[73] There were opportunities for this sort of discussion in the winter work of "paving" potatoes, that is, turning seed potatoes so the sprits would all grow upwards.[74]

There were some limited local disputes that led to strike action, but nothing that led to permanent organisation.[75] A similar lack of interest was demonstrated towards the introduction of parish councils. Whilst for some these bodies were the coming of democracy to the village, in general their limited finances ensured their failure to live up to expectations. The first election in 1894, however, was taken very seriously by both owner and agent in Speke. Miss Watt felt that what she called a "representative labourer" was needed on the Council – "a steady, well behaved man, of course, and not a political agitator". Graves was in agreement but was despondent as to the chances of finding a suitable candidate. "Where in this Township does he reside?" he asked, "If once you get one placed on the council, the agitator will soon be with him and they will put who they choose on the council, it will not be left for us to make the selection".[76] It is difficult to say whether there was political discussion amongst the labourers or whether the fears of "agitators" were just paranoia on the estate's part. In the event no labourers at all turned up to the election meeting. A similar indifference was displayed across the rest of the plain. At Tarleton, however, Richard Yates stood as the "Labour candidate" on the Nonconformist slate. This slate was successful at the first meeting, but the election was held again and a Church slate returned.[77] Elections for parish councils were by show of hand at open meetings, and it is possible that this was the reason for the seeming indifference of the labourers. The General Elections held after the franchise was extended to some labourers, and conducted by secret ballot, did not see an end to the Tory dominance of the area. (If the Speke experience is reliable, estates spent much effort ensuring that labourers would vote the "right" way).[78] There was perhaps the glimmer of a recognition of separate interests, but the development of this had to wait until the next century. Before that, we have to look at the events which led farmers towards their own independent organisations.

Notes
1. Dickson, *op. cit.*, p. 598.
2. T. E. Gibson, *Lydiate Hall*, London, 1876, p. 301.

3. *Orms. Adv.*, 9 January 1913.
4. Rothwell, *op. cit.*, pp. 126, 127.
5. *Ibid.*, appendix, p. 51. Cf. E. J. Hobsbawm and G. Rude, *Captain Swing*, Harmondsworth, 1973, p. 24.
6. J. D. Marshall, 'The Lancashire Rural Labourer in the Early Nineteenth Century', *Transactions of the Lancashire and Cheshire Antiquarian Society*, 71, 1961, pp. 100-5; Barnes, *Changes*, p. 59, 97; *Orms. Adv.*, 25 June 1857; *J.R.A.S.E.*, 1877, p. 465; Board of Trade, Report on Wages, Earnings and conditions of Employment of Agricultural Labourers in the U.K., 1905, Cd. 2376, App. V, p. 174.
7. Hale correspondence, 26 April 1872.
8. Binns, *op. cit.*, p. 138.
9. Rothwell, *op. cit.*, p. 130.
10. Hale correspondence, 30 September 1872.
11. DDSc 79/1/53, 21 May 1884.
12. DDLi: Steward's report for 1875. See also reports for 1874 and 1891.
13. *Orms. Adv.*, 15 May 1884. See also Derby diaries 16 January 1887 and Mutch, *Class and Paternalism, op. cit.*, for the mixed motivation in the rebuilding of cottages.
14. Mutch, *Mechanisations, op. cit.*
15. Gibson, *op. cit.*, p. 301. Cf. Hewittson, *op. cit.*, p. 234.
16. P.R.O. Census, 1871 RG/10/3870.
17. E. H. Hunt, 'Labour Productivity in British Agriculture 1850-1914', *Econ. Hist. Rev.*, 34, 1967, p. 280.
18. Speke papers 10/18, 8 October 1897.
19. The following account is based on the wages books of Mount Pleasant Farm, Speke, 1891 (920SPE 7/1) and Park Farm Rufford, 1871 (DDHe 62/63).
20. The importance of extra money at harvest time is stressed in Penn, *op. cit.*, p. 9.
21. *Orms. Adv.*, 24 July 1884.
22. Garnett, *op. cit.*, p. 14.
23. *Orms. Adv.*, 13 July 1893.
24. *Ibid.*, 26 July 1894.
25. Speke papers 10/5, 21 June 1896.
26. Interview, James Sephton, farmworker, started work 1925, father active in 1913 strike.
27. First Annual Report of the Committee of the Manchester Farmers' Club 1873, p. 15; Grundy, *op cit.*, p. 132.
28. Speke papers 10/4, 17 February 1888; 10/11, 29 October 1902.
29. *Orms. Adv.*, 16 January 1879.
30. *Ibid.*, 28 June 1913.
31. Marshall, *op. cit.*, p. 192; J. H. Nodal and G. Milner, *A Glossary of the Lancashire Dialect* (1875), Bath, 1972.
32. Rothwell, *op. cit.*, app., p. 51.
33. P.R.O. Census 1851, Aughton, HO/107/2196; Rothwell, *op cit.*, app. p. 51.
34. R. C. Agriculture (1882), p. 665; Census, Sefton RG/10/3838.
35. Interview, James Sephton.
36. Speke papers, 10/7, 31 May 1896.
37. *Orms. Adv.*, 25 June 1891.
38. J. Handley, *The Irish in Modern Scotland*, Cork, 1947, p. 171.
39. E. J. T. Collins, "Migrant Labour in British Agriculture in the Nineteenth Century", *Econ. Hist. Rev.*, 29, 1976, p. 52.
40. *Orms. Adv.*, 17 September 1857, 22 July 1897.
41. R. C. Labour (Ire) PP 1893-4, c. 6894, XXXVII, p. 73.
42. Interview, John Blundell.
43. R. C. Labour (Ire), pp. 13-14.
44. *Manchester Guardian*, 31 August 1842.
45. Interview, James Sephton.
46. *Orms. Adv.*, 5 July, 16 August 1894.
47. *Ibid.*, 24 February 1887.
48. Barnes, *op. cit.*, p. 122.
49. Hawthorne, *op. cit.*, p. 430.
50. DDSc 108/2; Wages book, 1881; Speke papers, 7/1, Mount Pleasant Wages Book, 20 August 1892.
51. Speke papers, 10/6; 8 October 1891, 2 November 1891, 14 November 1892.
52. Hale correspondence, 1 May 1883, 6 May 1883.
53. Penn, *op. cit*, p. 122.
54. DDSc 127/3, 6 September 1783.

46

55. DDLi 78, Steward's report 1881; *Orms. Adv.*, 9 January 1879.
56. Derby Diaries, 24 January 1870.
57. DDHe 10437, Rufford Clothing Club 1845.
58. Hewittson, *op. cit.*, pp. 223-4.
59. Report of the Registrar of Friendly Societies, PP 1867 (515).
60. Hale correspondence, 13 August 1880.
61. Barnes, *Changes*, pp. 111-12.
62. *Orms. Adv.*, 31 July 1879.
63. *Ibid.*, 31 July 1884.
64. *Liverpool Review*, 8 August 1885.
65. W. Warburton, *Notes on Altcar Parish*, Liverpool, 1894, p. 40.
66. Hewittson, *op. cit.*, p. 218, 227.
67. *Orms. Adv.*, 27 August 1888.
68. Warburton, *op cit.*, p. 40.
69. *Ibid.*, pp. 41, 44. Cf. R. W. Malcolmson, *Popular Recreations in English Society 1700-1850*, Cambridge 1973.
70. DDSc 127/3, 17 April 1767, 10 April 1789.
71. G. C. Newstead, *Annals of Aughton*, Liverpool, 1893, p. 39.
72. J. Harland and T. T. Wilkinson, *Lancashire Folklore*, London, 1867, p. 228; cf. Barnes, *Changes*, p. 111.
73. Derby Diaries, 6 August 1872.
74. 920DER(15), 40/1, Lord Stanley's notebook, 12 January 1857.
75. R. Knappet, *A Pullet on the Midden*, London, 1946, p. 34.
76. As described in A. Mutch, "Lancashire's Revolt of the Field; the Ormskirk Farmworkers strike of 1913", *North West Labour History Society Bulletin*, 8, 1982-3, p. 57.
77. Speke papers, 13/8 14 July and 30 November 1894, 10/6 21 July and 5 December 1894.
78. *Orms. Adv.*, 29 November, 6 December, 20 December 1894.

Plate 3: Much of the milk supply of the urban areas was produced by town dairies, leaving the farmers of the plain to produce vegetables and grain for both human and animal populations

5

The Emergence of Conflict

(a) The end of prosperity? Agricultural depression in the 1890s

The rural economy underpinning the society described so far was an expanding and prosperous one. A slowly improving standard of living in the towns fed the urban demand that was the key to the area's prosperity. This in turn fuelled the process of reclamation. The beginning of victory over Marten Mere came with the installation of steam pumping engines in 1850. This was far from the end, however. Derby could still be criticised in 1891 for failing to reclaim his portion of the Mere.[1] Large sections of Chat and Carrington Mosses lay waste until Manchester Corporation bought them in 1895 and 1896 respectively. Thousands of tons of town waste were dumped on them, and the land turned into productive arable.[2] Thus it was that "this region alone in Britain acquired an increasing proportional area of arable land during the late nineteenth and twentieth centuries when in fact in the remainder of Britain arable was on the decline".[3] However, these years also saw a shock to the vision of endless prosperity that seemed at mid-century to be the farming future.

The rest of English farming had received this shock in the 1870s. It started with appalling weather but was deepened by increasing foreign competition, first from grain from America and secondly from meat carried in the new refrigerated ships from Australasia. The grain counties were faced with lower output and lower prices; many producers could not withstand the pressure and went out of business. As Lord Ernle, in a famous passage, put the situation:

> Since 1862 the tide of agricultural prosperity had ceased to flow; after 1874 it turned and rapidly ebbed. A period of depression began which, with some fluctuations in severity, continued throughout the rest of the reign of Queen Victoria, and beyond.[4]

This statement remained the consensus view of historians until challenged in the early 1960s by T. W. Fletcher. Drawing upon research in Lancashire, he argued firstly that contemporary writers and investigations were biased towards the corn growing counties and secondly, flowing from this, that the orthodoxy ignored the tremendous regional variation in British agriculture.[5] From a detailed study of Lancashire livestock farming in the period he concluded that the depth of the recession had been considerably exaggerated.[6] There is considerable force in Fletcher's warnings about the nature of the contemporary evidence. Clearly, with a very regionally differentiated agrarian economy, simplistic generalisations drawn from the experience of one region will hide the reality of a complex situation. However, in his anxiety to counter over-simplification he is guilty of overstating his case. The problem here lies not with the figures he presents, but with the interpretation they are made to bear. Contemporary complaints about

48

depression in Lancashire are written off as the usual grumbles to be expected of farmers. Tenant farmer movements are the unrepresentative moans of a "vociferous minority".[7] The impression is that, having proved to his own satisfaction that the price series are evidence enough that depression was shallow if present at all, Fletcher then convinced himself that contemporary statements to the contrary were almost worthless.

The problem is that estate correspondence indicates that both agents and owners, not men likely to take farmers' complaints at face value without supporting evidence, were worried about their tenants' situation. Fletcher did not study the south west, commenting that "As an example of pure arable farming that weathered the depression unchanged it merits separate treatment".[8] Examination of the evidence shows this comment to be wide of the mark.[9] To be sure, depression came much later to the area than to the rest of the country, but the 1890s gave a severe jolt to farmers' confidence. This shock had important social consequences, producing the tenant farmer movements which Fletcher dismisses so casually. In what follows, I want to argue that they represented an important shift in rural society. Depression is much more than hard economic data; it also involves peoples' perceptions of their situation. As P. J. Perry points out, "many farmers and landowners believed they were experiencing hard times whatever the objective reality of their position".[10] It is only from this starting point that one can make sense of the actions of south west Lancashire farmers in this period.

The crucial event was the coincidence in the 1890s of low prices for all the produce of the area's farms. Wheat had fallen steadily since the 1880s. Of more importance was the drop in prices for hay and straw, which reached lows in 1896 and 1895 respectively. Potatoes too came under pressure from imports, particularly the earlies which had been a staple of the area. As the Scarisbrick agent admitted, "ever since 1880 produce of all kinds has kept very low in price especially corn and potatoes on which this Estate is so dependent".[11] This was far from constituting a "Great Depression" but it did come as a psychological shock to farmers accustomed to steady prices and ample markets. In addition, the reaction of these farmers cannot be viewed out of context. They were well aware, through their newspapers and journals, of the disasters which had befallen their southern counterparts. They feared their future would be equally grim. Their fears may have been exaggerated, but this makes them nonetheless real.

The impact of falling prices hit the middling farmers hardest of all. Those small farmers who produced a wide range of vegetables were to a large extent cushioned against the worst effects. In addition, they generally relied on unpaid family labour. The simultaneous drop in price of those crops most widely grown meant that larger farmers were not so fortunate. One response was to attempt to carry more stock. As it got harder to obtain decent prices for hay and straw it seemed sensible to use it to keep stock, while at the same time taking advantage of the generally lower prices for animal feed. The main obstacle in the way of adoption of such a policy was the lack of adequate buildings. In Scarisbrick the agent reported that new buildings were required across the estate: "though the late tenants pressed for no improvements the new tenants have done so on the ground that they, turning their attention more to the rearing and breeding of stock cannot conveniently do without them".[12] Landlords were not always willing to meet this demand, fearing that another change in farming methods could result in unproductive expenditure.[13] The change to stock rearing thus required both farmers and landlords with capital and a willingness to invest. For this reason it was not an option open to all.

Other possible answers included increased mechanisation or a complete move.[14] Many Lancashire farmers found prosperity on farms vacated by bankrupt Essex men, rented cheaply from landlords desperate to get them off their hands.[15] All these solutions required capital and so were not open to many. Low prices over a number of years meant, reported John Betham, that "farmers have no doubt been expending their Capital to keep matters going". He also spoke of "(1) Want of Capital & (2) lack of confidence in laying out Capital" as factors contributing to farmers' problems.[16] Given that for many farmers any solution requiring substantial capital expenditure was out of the question, they were forced to look for relief in their major outlay: their rent.

The way in which such demands gathered momentum can be ascertained from a look at the experience on the Derby estates, largest in the area and the pacesetter for wider action. Calls for rent reductions began in the mid-1880s. In 1881 Derby was pleased to record that "The tenantry are content, they have suffered less than most: & on this side of the country I have no farms vacant".[17] By 1886, however, he was aware of the possibility that "some reduction on the agricultural parts of the estate will be necessary".[18] He still felt in 1888 that depression had had little effect, but he commented, "Still I shall have to make some reduction, if only because other landlords have done so, and it is now generally expected, and indeed I gave to the tenants on both days a kind of half promise of that sort, though in vague terms".[19] This drew protests from Sefton, "saying that he shall be compelled to the same, and that it will not be convenient".[20] Nevertheless a return of 10 per cent on the half-year's rent was sanctioned.

Even with reductions rents got harder to collect and arrears increased. In January 1890 rents collected from the Knowsley tenants were £5679 as against £6046 the previous year. As Derby acknowledged, "The year has been very unfavourable to them, for though crops have been good, prices are exceedingly low". The same story was repeated in Bickerstaffe and a reduction of 20 per cent on the next half-year's rent was promised. "I could see that it had been expected", he wrote, "and that there would have been disappointment if nothing of the kind had been promised".[21] This still did not ease matters, as in 1892 an entry notes: "Some of the farmers near Ormskirk have printed up and circulated a letter demanding a reduction of 25 per cent: this we decline, but promise them some relief". A further ten per cent abatement was sanctioned. Interestingly, he comments that these "come to less in reality than in appearance, for where rents are in arrears, as in the case of many small tenants they are, the arrear is deducted from the abatement, so that it only involves the sacrifice of an irrecoverable debt".[22]

50

(b) Tenant farmer organisations

Demands for rent reductions began in the mid-1880s and increased in number into the 1890s. By then they started to become the product of organised groups of farmers. The first approach of many farmers was on a parish or estate basis. Thus the petition of 68 tenants of the Scarisbrick Trustees for reduction or remission of rents read:

> Your Memorialists are not disposed to make the matter a subject of agitation or public controversy but on the other hand desire it to be understood that the movement has been initiated after grave deliberation . . . open and combined action (when rich and poor and great and small farmers suffer alike) is the proper course for them to take.[23]

Such concerted action was impossible for tenants on the vast "Great Estates". Others were worried about the problem of victimisation. Some landowners flatly refused to meet delegations, even those comprised solely of their own tenants. For these reasons, some farmers began to look towards new forms of organisation.

The organisations which existed fell far from meeting requirements. There was barely any alternative to the long-established agricultural societies. These, in the words of one critic, "reflected only the honour and the glory side of farming, the swagger and show of it".[24] Their concern was the annual show and technical improvements to land and stock; any hint of conflict was anathema to them. The exceptions to the general lack of farming organisations were two clubs set up in 1872. The Croxteth Farmers' Club, initially for tenants of the Earl of Sefton, was established by the agent, Colonel Wyatt. It widened its membership to become the North Haymarket Club, fighting many battles with Liverpool Corporation on behalf of farmers using that market. By the 1890s it was known as the Liverpool and District Farmers' club and, initially at least, was firmly wedded to a policy of cooperation with landowners, Wyatt remaining as patron.[25]

The other club arose out of a meeting to discuss "the Labour Question". This was greeted with suspicion by Derby's agent, Hale, who confessed "to being rather shy of such associations as the most active members are often those who possess the least commonsense". The proposal was that the club be called the "Liverpool and Manchester Farmers' Club and Chamber of Agriculture", and it was to be firmly based on a "landed interest" model. Its membership was to include all ranks of rural membership, with labourers being given free membership. Amongst its aims was the desire "To constitute a Court of Appeal or Arbitration for Consideration and settlement when desired of any matters of dispute between Landlord and Tenant or between Master and Labourer".[26]

Derby was not keen on this challenge to his authority, but there were advantages to be gained from involvement. As Hale explained, "I have a great faith in people being led right, and a good lead is important now, when there are so many ready to misrepresent and to mislead others. I shall at once withdraw if there is any attempt to depart from the course that has been laid down".[27] On this advice Derby reluctantly accepted the Presidency of the Club, "less from the expectation that any particular good will come out of it, than from the fear that it may get into worse hands".[28] The value of involvement was shown in 1873 when Hale reported

> We had a great talk at the "Farmers Club" yesterday which resulted in a resolution that it was neither necessary nor politic to seek for legislation at present on arrangements between Landlord & Tenants. The cloven foot was shown by those who promoted the discussion and more will probably be heard from them on the subject.[29]

As early as this there were farmers who were starting to question the nature of their relations with their landlords, but they were not strong enough to carry their position. Hale remained in firm control of the Club, steering it into the safer waters of discussion of technical questions, such as "Does the application of artificial manure or the frequent growth of corn deteriorate the land?"[30] Despite this, Lord Winmarleigh could talk despondently to Derby in 1882 about

> the temper of the farmers, who he thought were on the way to make the same demands as had been made in Ireland. There was no feeling against the gentry, he said, at present, but agitators were very busy, & they had their own way at farmers' meetings, where the gentry did not commonly attend.[31]

This may have been so, but these clubs were still under lordly patronage. They may have been prepared to lead battles against outside forces, but not to recognise the existence of splits within the 'farming interest'. The demand for rent reductions was one which presupposed different material interests. As such, it could not be prosecuted by existing clubs. What was required were clubs organised by farmers, to pursue ends determined by, and of benefit to, farmers themselves.

There had been a farmers' club in Ormskirk in 1865 to combat the great rinderpest outbreak, but it had disappeared sometime afterwards. It was re-established in early 1891 as the Ormskirk and District Farmers' Club and was a founder member of the National Federation of Tenant Farmers' Clubs in January 1893.[32] Before this it had issued the appeal turned down by Derby. Such rejection was a common response. Landowners saw any organisation as a challenge to their authority and insisted on dealing with farmers individually. This was the response of the Scarisbrick Trustees to the memorial from their own tenants. Clubs with a wider membership agitating for more general demands met with even firmer rejection. On the Sefton estates Wyatt refused in 1890 to meet a delegation from the Liverpool and District Farmers' Club to discuss possible rent reductions, but instead sent out a letter to one farmer in each township summoning them to a meeting, at which he offered a ten per cent return of rent or a permanent reduction of five per cent.[33] This was despite the fact that he himself had founded the club, of which Sefton was the president. Clearly he felt that the club should restrict itself to technical questions or disputes with Liverpool Corporation. In his opinion,

> Agitators and talkers in the ranks of agriculture seek to set tenants against landlords, and labourers against both, and draw a hard and fast line between them, whereas their interests are identical, and mutual confidence is their greatest security.

The remedy was "To endeavour to interest the Government to suppress agitators, clubs, and talking assemblies".[34]

His action was in response to a very mildly worded circular issued by the club asking that, in view of a "serious decrease in the prices of all agricultural produce without any corresponding reduction in the cost of cultivation", a return or reduction of rent be made. They further declared,

> that this meeting refrains from adopting any hard and fast line, feeling that such a procedure would be attended with inconvenience and might be construed as of an arbitrary character, and further feeling satisfied that under the circumstances an appeal in the direction indicated has only to be laid before the landowners in a fair and temperate manner to secure their favourable consideration.

This appeal was sent to 45 landowners; only six replied. Of these, three were acknowledgements, two indicated that they had already given abatements, and T. C. Mather of Liverpool declared that he was well aware of the drop in prices without the club's advice, and that he would deal with individual tenants when he felt this to be necessary.[35] It seems clear that landowners were not concerned with the specific content of appeals. Class organisation of any kind cut across the traditional bonds of rural society, and the response was to oppose it in whatever form it took, counterposing solutions based on individual estates or farmers. In one case the response went even further. The eviction of James Middlehurst briefly became something of a *cause celebre*. It is worthy of closer examination not least because the availability of estate papers shows how little reliance can be placed on their public pronouncements. For all their Olympian detachment, landowners were clearly worried by farmers' organisations, and were capable of considerable manipulation to rid themselves of danger.

We have already seen how Middlehurst put his beliefs in farmer self-organisation into practice by standing for Parliament in the 1892 General Election. He had been a committee member of the Liverpool and District Farmers' Club and was a founder member of the revived Ormskirk Club. In late 1892 he went as a delegate from the latter to the conference of the Central Chamber of Agriculture called to discuss the agricultural crisis. However, the conference proved an enormous disappointment. Instead of discussing questions of land tenure and rent reduction the conference was a carefully stage-managed display of support for Protection and class harmony. Middlehurst's verdict was "A ridiculous demonstration in favour of Protection, and, as no practical suggestions have emanated from it, a waste of time".[36] Soon after he also attended the founding conference of the National Federation of Farmers' Clubs. Here again he found himself in disagreement: "He could not say that he was in favour of a Land Court and the 3 'F's. He would prefer if possible to secure an amendment of the Agricultural Holdings Act". To this end he proposed a resolution that the movement "should look for a remedy of the present state of things in a measure of compulsory compensation for unexhausted improvements, the abolition of the law of distress and the division of local rates", which found little support.[37]

Middlehurst was an articulate exponent of tenant farmers' causes and certainly no lover of landlords, but he was not on the radical wing of the movement. Despite this, a few weeks after he had attended the conference together with three other tenants from the Scarisbrick estate, he received notice to quit his farm.

John Betham, the agent, phrased it as follows: if Middlehurst was dissatisfied with his farm, the estate would take it off his hands. According to him Middlehurst "replied that he certainly was dissatisfied, making certain mis-statements in his reply, and the Trustees gave him notice to quit".[38] He amplified this in a newspaper interview:

> Mr Middlehurst says that he had an intimation that if he didn't give up the farm he would receive a notice to quit. Why, we never even thought of it at all. We first of all ask him, after seeing those statements, if he is dissatisfied with the farm, and if he is we tell him frankly that we are willing to take it off his hands.[39]

However, it is clear from a letter from the Trustees that they were determined to be rid of Middlehurst. In it they gave Betham the text of the letter to be sent to Middlehurst and the instruction that "unless he admits in writing before the 30th inst that he has no cause of complaint he be served with notice to quit before the 2nd prox".[40] The Trustees must have been well aware that a man of Middlehurst's temperament could give no such assurance. Indeed a letter from Betham to the *Bolton Chronicle* has them shifting their ground and letting slip the reason behind their action:

> We never interfere with our tenants attending any meeting they like. I have endeavoured all along in the letters which have been published to show that the reason Mr Middlehurst got notice to quit was because he complained about and was dissatisfied with his farm. His *persistent agitation* would have been the means of causing dissatisfaction amongst the other tenants on the estate who are perfectly satisfied and content.[41]

After this even Forwood, who had no cause to favour Middlehurst, concluded that "The reason for giving Mr Middlehurst notice to quit was not his conduct as a farmer, or want of punctuality in payment of his rent, but simply some expressions in public at an agricultural meeting in Chester".[42]

The Trustees' worries about other farmers being infected by Middlehurst's dissatisfaction extended to other estates. Thus Betham wrote to a neighbouring landowner, J. Munford, warning him of

> the trouble we are having with Mr Middlehurst who farms Berry House on the Scarisbrick Trust Estate. It is not at all unlikely that the same kind of agitation which he is doing his best to foster will extend to your Estate. I would like in a friendly way to point out to you that a great deal of this agitation in the immediate district originates at the Swan Hotel Bescar Lane.[43]

The wider impact of the Estates' actions were clearly grasped by at least one other member of the local ruling class. The Rev. R. C. Fletcher of Tarleton wrote to congratulate Charles Scarisbrick, saying that "You have made it abundantly plain that there is an owners as well as a tenants version of the agricultural position, and the landowners as a class owe you a debt of gratitude for doing so".[44]

Farmers by no means saw things as clearly. The Liverpool club expelled Middlehurst because his speech at Chester was one "likely to cause & produce bad feeling between Landlord & Tenant".[45] Support from local farmers was also patchy. Petitions were signed by at least 109 tenants showing their "disapproval of the present agitation caused by Mr James Middlehurst" and acknowledging

54

"their appreciation of the fair treatment we have always received".[46] Middlehurst alleged that the farmer who organised this was " 'ashamed and very sorry to do what he is doing", but, as he has said, 'the paper was forced upon him and he dared not refuse to take it!' "[47] Support for this view can be found in the fact that the text of the petition is amongst the estate papers, together with a list of "Tenants who up to this March 20 1893 have not been asked to sign paper".[48] Despite this estate manipulation, there is little doubt that there was hostility to Middlehurst. A "Banks Farmer" argued that the problem lay with "outsiders" who took farms because they could offer more rent. He went on to claim that when they got into difficulties:

> They either become dissatisfied and turn agitator for the redress of grievances which are often more imaginary than real, or like men they honourably give up their farms and thus make room for more practical men. I am afraid we must class Mr J. Middlehurst among the former.[49]

Middlehurst had failed to shake more than a minority of farmers from their unswerving loyalty to their landlords. In the words of the "Banks Farmer", "Banks farmers are scarcely so changeable in their esteem for their landlords as some are". Faced with this lack of support Middlehurst accepted his eviction and moved to Essex in the footsteps of so many Lancashire farmers. He prospered there and continued for a time to bombard the *Ormskirk Advertiser* with his views.[50]

Middlehurst's case illustrates that farmers were far from a homogeneous group with the same interests or perceptions. Opposition to the new organisations amongst farmers came from two quarters. On the one hand were the "small yet powerful minority of Lancashire farmers whose past accumulations had put then in such a position that they were practically independent of their farms".[51] Farmers like these were organised in the Liverpool club and shaped its initial policy of support for the landowners. On the other hand were the small farmers whose loyalty to landlords we have already noted. For these men the response to depression was to tighten the belt another notch. Interestingly, the "Banks Farmer" was a man who also carried out building work for the estate.[52] Both large and small farmers had strategies for riding out depression. It was the middling farmers, with no alternative sources of finance, who turned to organisation. It is noticeable, however, that the appeal to the Scarisbrick Trustees quoted above was presented in 1896 by all classes of farmer on the estate. Events conspired to push farmers together, although too late to save Middlehurst.

The impact of Middlehurst's eviction was to set back the cause of tenant farmer organisation. His successor as Ormskirk delegate to the Lancashire Tenant Farmers' Association, James Sephton, complained that "farmers in his district could not be persuaded to say in public what they said at their own fireside. He thought at heart they believed in the organisation but they would not openly support it".[53] The Estate had succeeded in not only removing a nuisance but also in deterring others. Organisation was further undermined by the change in the conditions which had called it into being. There was widespread granting of rent reductions (attributed by James Sephton to Middlehurst's work and by other tenant farmers' leaders to a desire by landlords to head off their demands) and prices began to improve gradually into the early 1900s.

The Ormskirk club carried on, but changed its allegiance in 1902 by joining forces with the North Lancashire Farmers' Association to form the Lancashire Farmers' Association. The N.L.F.A. had its origins in the Fylde on the instigation of the local landowner, Fitzherbert-Brockholes. It was bitterly attacked by the proponents of tenant farmer organisation as being a 'Landlord's Association'.[54] However, the Lancashire Tenant Farmers' Association shrank to its base among the small dairy farmers of North East Lancashire. By the end of 1908 the L.F.A. claimed over 2,300 members in 30 branches and north-east Lancashire clubs began to affiliate.[55]

The attempt to build separate tenant farmers' organisations failed to attract anything more than a minority of the area's farmers. It is arguable that many joined because of short term fears rather than because they had any belief in the ideas being propounded by their leaders. When the immediate danger had passed they turned to other organisations. However, the fact that they joined any organisation marks a change. It was also the case that these organisations had themselves changed under the impact of the radicals. Thus, it has been seen that the Liverpool club was a firm proponent of landlord-tenant co-operation. Its chairman argued in 1890 that "So far as the club was concerned, it was useful as a body between bodies, but it would be better to keep out of private contracts".[56] By 1895 the club had issued a circular calling for a permanent reduction in rents and, in the election of that year, had sent a questionnaire to all candidates asking if they would promote land tenure reform.[57] In the same way the L.F.A. encompassed both farmer and landlord, but the leadership had shifted towards the former. Through their organisations farmers were demanding a greater share in the leadership of rural society. While the tenant farmer organisations lost their exclusive nature at the end of the century, farmers' organisations continued, led by farmers. The matters discussed were wider than the annual show, and landlords, if involved, were members as *farmers* rather than as patrons. In this way the organisations were forerunners of the National Farmers' Union, and their emergence represents a change in the nature of rural society, cutting across the traditional bonds fostered by landlords.

(c) The revolt of the field, 1913

This change was seen in practice when the next crack in the edifice of the "landed interest" emerged. In the farm workers' strike of 1913 it was the farmers who took the lead. Derby was relegated to the role of conciliator, "stating that if his services could be of any use in any way the farmers had only to command them".[58] Fitzherbert-Brockholes, still President of the L.F.A., recommended "an exchange of ideas between the farm workers and the farmers with a view to trying to get at what might be reasonable grievances on the part of the men".[59] This advice was rejected in favour of an attempt to "squash" the union, the approach favoured by local farmers. In Speke it was recognised that rather than

56

the estate following its own policy, "it is much better to support the farmers in whatever they determine". The extent to which the estate's sway over the farmers had crumbled is revealed in the agent's despairing comment in 1915, "I have consulted the farmers in Speke, and I am just as convinced as I was two years ago at the time of the strike, that it is only a waste of time in doing so, they all have different methods . . . they as a rule tell you one thing, and fully agree with what you propose, but follow their own ideas at the end".[60]

It could be argued that the farmers' break with landowners encouraged farm workers to look to their own interests. Certainly when they decided to act for themselves the change came in spectacular style. The strike has been described in detail elsewhere, but basically it showed a high level of organisation, with flying pickets and cycle patrols.[61] It saw considerable violence as strikers clashed with police escorting food convoys into Liverpool. Victory came thanks to solidarity action by industrial workers, chiefly railwaymen.

What was the cause of "one of the strongest conflicts in modern industrial warfare", as the *Manchester Guardian* described the strike?[62] The growth of farmers' organisations may have prompted farm workers to look to organise themselves. There had also been long-term changes in their position: the move from farm servants to labourers; the increase in mechanisation; the decline in the importance of casual migrant labour; and, according to farmers, the impact of education which caused the loss of "pride in the land and that love of stock which prompted his forefathers to render willing and humble sacrifice to the farmers".[63] However, these underlying trends are inadequate explanations. There was an immediate economic motive in the failure of wages to keep pace with the steady increase in prices. But the major reason must be sought in the wider industrial context. The years from 1910 to 1914 were the years of the "great labour unrest". Union membership leapt from 2,477,000 at the end of 1909 to 4,135,000 at the end of 1913. Total strikes reached a peak of 1,497 in 1913, and over 40,915 strike days were recorded in 1912.[64] Amongst these were some titanic national struggles, notably by transport workers. However, the period saw unionism and industrial action spreading through whole new sections of the working class. This massive rise in the confidence of the working class to take matters into their own hands, often against union leaderships, spilled over to the farm workers. Mass industrial action was seen as a credible means of winning demands. However, to this mood of confidence has to be added organisation. This was supplied by two railway workers, G. A. Newman and John Phipps. They were free from the constraints on farm workers, but at the same time an integral part of the local economy, which relied heavily on rail transport. They were also both revolutionary socialists, who were able to have their concepts of rank and file self-organisation adopted by the strikers. They were even able to hold farm workers after the strike to their model of trade unionism, a model which was opposed by the leadership and led to the formation of a breakaway union. Of course, their lead was accepted within limits. This showed itself in farm workers' opposition to the verbal attacks made on Lord Derby by other trade unionists. However the verdict of the Speke agent on the consequences of the dispute were that the workers were "difficult to manage and are influenced to a great extent by Agitators against doing their duty to their employers".[65]

The outbreak of war in 1914 was such a massive break that it is pointless to project what might have happened to farm workers had it not occurred. They certainly began to enjoy higher wages, thanks to labour scarcity. Their new union, the Farm and Dairy Workers Union, spread its influence into Cheshire and North Wales before merging with the Workers' Union in 1918. This success was to be shortlived, however, as agriculture was hammered by economic depression and the labour market was swollen by the urban unemployed. The period since the Second World War has seen a dramatic increase in farm amalgamations and in the rate of agricultural productivity. Farm workers continue, however, to be amongst the lowest paid in British industry.

Notes

1. *Orms. Adv.*, 22 January 1891.
2. A. H. Fitton, "Farming the Mosslands of Lancashire", *J.R.A.S.E.*, 1965, p. 71.
3. J. A. Taylor, *Studies in South West Lancashire Agriculture*, London, 1964, p. 3.
4. Lord Ernle, "The Great Depression and Recovery 1874-1914", in P. J. Perry (ed.), *British Agriculture 1875-1914*, London, 1973, p. 1.
5. T. W. Fletcher, "The Great Depression of English agriculture 1873-1896", in Perry, *op. cit.*, pp. 30-55.
6. T. W. Fletcher, "Lancashire Livestock Farming during the Great Depression", in Perry, *op. cit.*, pp. 76-108.
7. *Ibid.*, p. 99.
8. *Ibid.*, p. 78.
9. I have presented the detailed economic evidence for what follows in A. Mutch, "Farmers' Organisations and Agricultural Depression in Lancashire 1890-1900", *Agricultural History Review*, 31, 1983. This account concentrates on developing the discussion of the social consequences.
10. P. J. Perry, *British Farming in the Great Depression*, Newton Abbot, 1974, p. 183.
11. DDSc 127/8, Papers prepared by John Betham, agent, relating to agricultural depression, report to trustees.
12. DDSc 79/1/47, Report . . . on new farm buildings required, 22 May 1882.
13. Speke papers, 13/9, 13 May 1895.
14. *Preston Guardian*, 20 April 1895.
15. Smith, *op cit*.
16. DDSc 127/8, Betham's report.
17. Derby Diaries, 1 January 1881.
18. *Ibid.*, 2 January 1886.
19. *Ibid.*, 11 January 1888.
20. *Ibid.*, 29 January 1888.
21. *Ibid.*, 7, 8, 21 January 1890.
22. *Ibid.*, 13 November, 14 December 1892.
23. DDSc 127/18, 16 September 1896.
24. *Preston Guardian*, 11 February 1893.
25. *Orms. Adv.*, 16 February 1872, 21 February 1878, 17 February 1881, 10 March 1887, 22 November 1888.
26. Hale correspondence, 26 April, 11 May 1872.
27. *Ibid.*, 15 June 1872.
28. Derby Diaries, 17 June 1872.
29. Hale correspondence, 3 April 1873.
30. *Orms. Adv.*, 28 March 1878.
31. Derby Diaries, 3 October 1882.
32. *Orms. Adv.*, 19 February 1891.
33. *Ibid.*, 22 May 1890.
34. R. C. Agriculture, Report, pp. 17, 46.

58

35. *Orms. Adv.*, 17 April, 22 May 1890.
36. *Ibid.*, 15 December 1892.
37. *Agricultural Gazette*, 10 January 1893, p. 58.
38. *Preston Guardian*, 25 February 1893.
39. *Ibid.*, 18 February 1893.
40. DDSc 79/1/53, "re Middlehurst, Berry House", 19 January 1893.
41. Cited in *Preston Guardian* 11 March 1893. Betham had conveniently forgotten the three other Scarisbrick tenants who had attended the conference with Middlehurst.
42. *Orms. Adv.*, 10 August 1893.
43. DDSc 79/1/53, 18 February 1893.
44. *Ibid.*, 17 February 1893.
45. *Ibid.*, 18 March 1893.
46. *Ibid.*, March 1893.
47. *Orms. Adv.*, 16 March 1893.
48. DDSc 79/1/53.
49. *Orms. Adv.*, 16 March 1893.
50. *Ibid.*, 2 November 1893; *Preston Guardian,* 9 June 1894.
51. *Preston Guardian*, 2 May 1896.
52. *Orms. Adv.*, 23 March 1893.
53. *Preston Guardian*, 3 March 1894.
54. *Ibid.*, 26 May 1900.
55. *Preston Herald*, 25 January, 1 February, 4 April, 12 December 1908.
56. *Orms. Adv.*, 22 May 1890.
57. *Ibid.*, 14 November 1895; *Preston Guardian*, 1 February 1896.
58. *Times*, 24 May 1913.
59. *Ibid.*
60. Speke papers, 10/14, 14 and 17 June 1913, 25 February 1915.
61. Mutch, *Lancashire's Revolt of the Field, op. cit.*
62. *Manchester Guardian*, 24 June 1913.
63. *Orms. Adv.*, 9 January 1913.
64. B. Holton, *British Syndicalism 1900-1914*, London, 1976.
65. Speke papers, 10/14, 7 October 1913.

Conclusion

The rural society that has been described was very different from that in much of the rest of England and indeed from parts of the north. It was an area above all dominated by the market. Its farming sytems were geared to meeting the enormous urban demand that lay on its doorstep. This was not the carefully balanced, long-term system of classical English mixed farming, with the market at a discrete distance. Crops were realised immediately for cash, which was used to replenish the soil. Following from this, it was a high rent, high wage district. However, these features were variations on the basic pattern which underlay the whole of English rural society, albeit expressed in an extreme form. The countryside was still controlled by a handful of extremely rich men, and the farm workers still worked long arduous hours for little reward. This allows us to pose some comparisons with the rest of the country.

Landowners in Lancashire were not as successful as they might have liked in directing rural affairs, but they strained hard to do so. Their actions were not those of disinterested grandees, but of men who intended to have their way, by manipulation and coercion if necessary. They rarely needed to resort to these, as for the most part they retained the loyalty of their tenants. However, when resistance came it flared up just as much in the "closed" parishes as elsewhere. The historical record gives the impression that dissent was limited to the open parishes like Headington Quarry. Perhaps the example of Speke was echoed in other parts. The dichotomy between "open" and "closed" parishes can at times blur the far more fundamental divide between landlord and landless.

It is evident that there were divisions amongst the area's farmers, divisions which led to the disunity of the 1890s. Small farmers were in the majority in south west Lancashire, but their importance has been underplayed in much rural history. They were not only socially important, but economically important too. The large progressive farmers were not always as successful as contemporary eulogies would have us believe. Whilst doubt has been expressed as to the accuracy of the term "peasant" in this context, it is clear that more work is required on the way in which varying fractions of the farming class interacted.

The Lancashire farm workers played no part in the great upheavals of the 1870s that play such a dominant role in labour history. Perhaps that indicates the weight of the Webb tradition, the view that sees labour history as the history of formal trade union structures. The events of 1913 indicate that a more fruitful approach would be to concentrate attention on the conflicts that arose in specific areas, and the ways in which these were resolved.[1]

Above all, I hope to have demonstrated that rural south west Lancashire was not the rural idyll of stability and harmony that the rural nostalgia merchants would have us accept. It was a society lived in by people with widely different interests, all of whom were subject to the forces of change, and who reacted in different ways according to their perceptions of the situation. The way in which we approach our past shapes our actions in the present. Those who argue for change in the modern countryside will, I hope, find some encouragement in the knowledge that change was won in the past.

Notes
1. For a splendid example, see A. Howkins, *Poor Labouring Men, Rural Radicalism in Norfolk 1870-1923*, London, 1985.

Plate 4: The Melling brass band, who led the procession of striking farm workers to Downholland in 1913 in protest against the eviction of union members from their cottages